CLAY AIKEN:

EVERYTHING
YOU'VE
EVER
WANTED
TO
KNOW
ABOUT
THE
NEW
SINGING
SENSATION

OTHER BOOKS BY GAYE DEAMER:

Commercal Foods Exposed!—And How To Replace Them

Help! Help! It's Egg Momelet

Wallpaper Cookies

Polka Dots and Paint

Jangeo— The Jovial Giraffe (Children's art book)

Forthcoming book:

PARENTS AND KIDS, SAY—"NO MORE!"
(A book in support of a Revolution For Decency.")

CLAY AIKEN:

EVERYTHING
YOU'VE
EVER
WANTED
TO
KNOW
ABOUT
THE
NEW
SINGING
SENSATION

THE UNAUTHORIZED BIOGRAPHY

GAYE DEAMER

PUBLISHING HOUSE

SALT LAKE CITY, UTAH

CLAY AIKEN: EVERYTHING YOU'VE EVER WANTED TO
KNOW ABOUT THE NEW SINGING SENSATION
by Gaye Deamer
Published by:
Publishing House
Post Office Box 540508
No. Salt Lake, Utah 84054-0508

Place orders: www.publishinghouse.biz

ISBN 1-932280-61-8   (hardcover)
Library Of Congress...2004114517
Gaye Deamer, author of   Clay Aiken: Everything You've Ever
Wanted To Know About The New Singing Sensation is not affiliated
in any way with Clay Aiken, 19 Entertainment, The Firm, FOX,
American Idol, or Freemantle Media.

Photography: Geoffrey Graybeal and Digital Wizards
Photography collages and blends: Bonnie Wallace
Artwork: Michael Morgan and Brian Charlesworth
Cover Design: Jeremy Bailey

CONTENTS

To Clay Holmes Aiken—For having the courage to say, "Not with me and not with my music."

To the indomitable Clay Aiken fans for their resolve to support decency and for the infinite hours of entertainment.

To Ina Deamer—A mother who everyone deserves, but I was somehow blessed. I am grateful for her incredible example and for being my best friend.

For Heidi and Brett; Mike and Marty; Mark and Courtney and for Joshua, Hope, Taylor, Paige, and Amber— who are   precious reminders as a single parent, I took parenting seriously.

Blends Created By Bonnie Wallace

To Gina
All my Love

ACKNOWLEGEMENTS

For fifteen months of 24/6, I have logged thousands of hours of research, interviews, writing, re-research and rewriting, because Clay Aiken's life just keeps unfolding. There are so many people who participated in the compilation of this book that it is impossible to give personal credit to everyone. Your input was instrumental in painting the picture of the real Clay Holmes Aiken. Heartfelt thanks is extended to many of Clay Aiken's friends, associates, co-workers and a myriad of other people whose names could not be mentioned (you know of your contribution) and your input is deeply appreciated.

My deepest gratitude:

To Literary Agent, Bob Silverstein. He likes spunk. I have appreciated his kind, yet no-nonsense direction and his two pages of one-liners with detailed instructions of what is required to write about celebrity— yet he never discouraged latitude. To Agent Jeff Kleinman—for his e-mail that said, "You write beautifully." I taped those three words in front of my computer when I was required to erase half of my manuscript to stay within my First Amendment Rights—also when I was on my fourth rewrite and on those days when I questioned my resolve—I would read those three words, and start again. (Authors will understand.) To Geoffrey Graybeal—gifted writer and Journalist. For our umpteen e-mails, phone conversations and for his great input and photography that introduced me to Clay's world in Raleigh, North Carolina. To David Laxton, Director of Communications at The Autism Society Of North Carolina for the detailed information. To Michael Morgan—the creative artist whose caricatures captured the humorous sides of Clay and his sidekicks. To Katie Brogan, Editor of Writer's Market for taking my phone calls in the midst of demanding schedules and for her instruction. To the bright and resilient Mary Ann Pedersen for her stellar eye and for the hours of painstaking editing and critiques. To Jeff Lambson, Jon Samuelson and Jeremy Bailey for their guidance and their publishing expertise. To Ryan Redmond for his generous creative computer assistance. To Heather McVey—assistant to Richard Paul Evans, for her help and enthusiasm. To The Digital Wizards whose click, click clicks provided hundreds of photographs—capturing every flutter of Clay Aiken's TV appearances and concerts. To Bonnie Wallace for her giving heart and for her beautiful photography collages and blends that capture the essence of Clay Aiken. To Legal Counsel and others who have helped me through the process. To my friends and family including Allen and Mary Cluer for your support in my life and for always being there.

To Aiken4U, Airplay Central, About You, Albany Times Union, Alexandra Corbin, All About Clay, All Things Clay Aiken, Amazon.com, Associated Press, Autism Society of American, Autism Society of North Carolina, BBC News, Beavers On Idol, Biblical Recorder, Billboard Magazine, Billboard Radio, Blake and Julie Murdock, Bolt Board, Brian Charlesworth, Buffalo News, C Acknowledgements, Canada AM, Carolina News, CBS News, Charlotte Observer, Chart Attach Toronto, Chicago Tribune, Chris Scheihing, Cincinnati Enquirer, Clayaiken, Clayaikenonline, Clayaikentheidealidol, Cathy, Claynadians, Claymaniacs, Clay MultiMedia Online, Cle Picket & Web Staff, Claytonaiken, Clay Aiken Fan, Clay Broadcast Network, Clay Forums, Cleveland Beakon Journal, CNN Headline News, CTV.CA, Daily Gazette, Daily Nebraskan, Dave and Geri-95.7 WLTH-Grand Rapids, David Blooomberg, David LaWrence Dewey, Deseret News, Diane and Mike Bubel, Drudge Report, Elle Magazine, Elites TV, Entertainment Tonight, Entertainment Weekly, Eva Simpson, EzBoard, Finding Clay Aiken, Fox 9 News, Foxes On Idol, Geocities, Good Morning America, Herald Sun, Hit makers

Honolulu Star Bulletin, Idolforums.com, Indy Star, Indianapolis Star Review, Innovations, Jagger and Kristi-94.1 FM, James McQuire, Jessica Callan, Jim Amato, Julian Bach, Kelcy Carlson, Magazine, Marraccini, Promo Innovations, Jan Mitchel, Jansjoyous Jungle, Kurt Jensen, KE Alaka'I, LA Times, Larry King Live, Leigh Dyer, Lycos 50, Mary Ann Lape, Melissa Ruggieri, Miami Herald, Michigan News, Minneapolis, Mod Bee, MSNBC, MTV, News 14 Carolina, News Observer, Newsweek, New York Post, New York Times, Niki Waldegrave, Orange County Register, Palm Beach Post, People Magazine, Platinum Celebrity Magazine, Pollstar, Promo Innovations, Radio Stations, Reality TV, Red Hot Topic, Richmond Times, Dispatch, Rolling Stone magazine, Ronnie Wolmack, Sacticket, Salt Lake City Tribune, Seattle Times, Sirlinksalot, Southern Baptist News, Spudroom, St. Paul Star Tribune, Star Tribune, Stephen M. Silverman, The Clay Board, The Clay Train Connection, The Ideal Idol, The Indy Channel, The People's Republic of Clay, That's The Clay, The Daily Record NC, The TV Column, Times, Times-Dispatch, Trenyce, USA Today, Victoria Strauss, Wilkes-Barre, Market, Times Leader, Washington Post, Whats Gonzo, WRAL TV, Writer's Yahoo, YMCA A. Finley, Zap it.E.

Bonnie Wallace

FORWARD

I never intended to write a book about Clay Aiken. However, I was entranced by the tender predicament he found himself in with *American Idol*. He lost the crown but won the hearts of millions of fans by serenading us with his beautiful voice. I have never participated in chat rooms but one day I Googled his name and found that thousands of others were also googled.... The talk from his fans was giggly and yearning. He awakened a thousand senses from every age—some flirtatious sensitivity that had been hidden and often entombed. The questions swirling about Clay Aiken were desperate and persistent—"Oh, I wish I knew this about him and I wish I knew that." My enthusiasm also wanted to know *this* and *that* and as a researcher and writer, my interest started surveying his past. I started to record my discovery—the fascination grew and my infatuation gradually required a binding.

However, the typical biography is written from research, interviews and offers editorial reporting. The biographer is an outsider who doesn't enter the story and doesn't get involved emotionally. I have spent thousands of hours in research and interviews for this book. In addition, I knew in writing Clay Aiken's story, this book could not be a typical biography because as a breathless supporter, I became involved in his emotional journey and was an active participant in his rise to fame. This book is written from that perspective. I know his fans so well because I am one of them. His fans do not want an editorial report; they want his emotional life story sometimes told poetically, yet garnished with a fountain of fun—because that is Clay Aiken. This book was written for them, while desiring to satisfy their age spans from 9 to 90 years old. As a result the book includes what his fans want: a detailed chronology of his life before *American Idol*; a replay of the peaks and valleys during his rise to fame; some flag waving—for someone who has the courage to make a difference; also humor, coupled with amusing caricatures; amazing photographs and much more...

Before I started the research, I did not know the real Clay Aiken.... I do now. My admiration and respect for Clay Holmes Aiken is indelible. I have never witnessed anyone who has accomplished so much in so few short years. Astounding! The book describes the depth of his participation in life. I have never seen anything like it. Enjoy, because I think you will be as enamored as I still am.

CHAPTER ONE

I just want to change the world somehow.

—Clay Aiken

THE PHENOMENAL RISE OF A
SINGING SENSATION

Lionel Richey, guest celebrity judge of *American Idol*, asked Clayton Holmes Aiken the question millions of fans are also asking? "Who Are you?"

Mr. Richey and Aiken's growing legion of fans want to know who is this Special Education Major who has captured the hearts of women and the respect of men of every age around the world? Yes, the world!

Clay Aiken's popularity grew as millions of viewers watched him battle his way through the trenches (out of 70,000 applicants) to capture the title as the 2nd Runner Up on the hit Reality TV show, *American Idol*. However, being crowned as the 2nd place winner has raised many eyebrows because his popularity has totally eclipsed the AI winner. Clay's single, "This Is The Night/ Bridge Over Troubled Water," was the top selling single of 2003. His album "Measure Of A Man," went double platinum (two-million shipped) its first week in release and topped the Billboard 100 Chart. His single "The Way/Solitaire" topped impressive sales in 2004. Plus *Rolling Stone* offered a cover shoot before his album was even released and he has been on the cover of most entertainment magazines.

No one has been more surprised from the international adulation than Clay Aiken. His fans are not only captivated by his incredible voice they have fallen in love with this true gentleman. Regardless, the worldwide attention has been overwhelming for this recent college graduate whose future was programmed to tutor kids with special needs. A young man who admitted he had not ventured very far from his familial roots in Raleigh, North Carolina.

Well the tables have turned—or let it be said—the desks have been turned upside down because Clay Aiken's life will never be the same. He will teach all right, but not in a normal 26-seated classroom with chalkboards, school books, and burning-the-midnight-oil, grading papers. He will burn-the-midnight-oil jetting from city to country, entertaining his fans from around the world.

Experience teaches that fame is fleeting; therefore Clay's teachings through precept and example will give him his most enduring audience and his most lasting applause.

Clay Aiken is genuine. What a refreshing change after having the degradation of the Entertainment Industry shoved down our unsuspected throats—that give us the Rap trash who regurgitate notes of societies filth and call it music.... Many consumers refuse to spend money on the entertainment menagerie who scream obscenities at the world and expect reimbursement for their debasement. We yearn for decency on a grand euphonious scale. Then Clay Holmes Aiken walks on Stage and his performance funnels through an aortic valve, allowing flow through our musically jaded hearts.

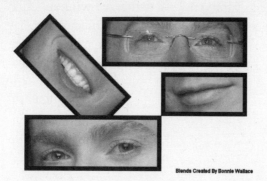

Blends Created By Bonnie Wallace

That voice, his wit and his charm are endearing—but there is something else—those eyes. His sea of green eyes are fringed with a layer of long shaded lashes you normally would-n't notice, but you notice and you can't help but scrutinize their performance.

Eyes are windows—they interpret the soul—some are abused, drugged, cruel, kind, unoccupied and some are worn with age. Clay's eyes are crystal and clear—his calliope of enticement. He and the cameras offer their invitation, and we accept and follow their gaze.

Then...there's that voice. Superlatives tempt, because there is no other way to explain it. Clay Aiken's performance is so tempting, when he opens his mouth in song, you merely stop what you are doing and you record your reaction. Then you keep rewinding and you keep listening. Somehow you can't get enough of his music that appears to be sung so effortlessly. As a result, many consumers who had stopped buying CD's, are willing to wait in zigzagged lines to buy photocopies of "that voice."

Clay's life and upbringing are so well grounded; he has obviously chosen to keep his musical journey on a higher ground. Clay has refused to participate in the dark side—the corruptible side of the entertainment industry that can lure true talents into prostituting their gifts.

Therein lies the key. His fans are investing in the package that is Clay Aiken. Because of him once-wary consumers are buying music again. Clay Aiken is making a difference. And clearly his fans are eager to support him in that quest.

For the rest of the Clay Aiken journey....

Bonnie Wallace

CHAPTER TWO

The childhood shows the man,
as morning shows the day.

Milton-Paradise Regained

CLAYTON GRISSOM—A YOUNG CHARMER

American Idol celebrity judge Gladys Knight said to Clay Aiken, "You are a mystery." Then G. McCarthy wrote, "There's something mystical about his face, like he sprung up—giggling from behind a toadstool in Tolkien's forest."

This mystical man was Clayton Grissom. When he was 20 years old he changed his name to Clayton Aiken—to his mother's maiden name, to erase the baggage of an abusive alcoholic father. *American Idol* show producers suggested he shortened his name to Clay—an easier fit with Aiken. However, his name has not only changed—since he was introduced on *American Idol*, Clay has transformed from the show's lanky "nerd" to his fan's label of "Irresistible Beast." This gentle yet spirited beast when adorned with such labels, raises his eyebrows with bewilderment and responds, "I can't figure it out!"

He also confirmed, "My appearance has changed, but I haven't changed. The wrapping on the package is different, but the gift is the same." Let's go back and examine the gift and unwrap Clayton Grissom/Clay Aiken's life.

Faye Aiken met Vernon Grissom in the late 70's when a group of musicians were putting a local band together. The newly formed band consisted of singer Faye Aiken; singer/guitarist Vernon Grissom; guitarist Wade Harris and drummer Billy Winston. Vernon, 11 years older than Faye, was a country singer and guitarist—his goal was to one-day sing at "The Grand Old Opry." While performing in the band, Vernon and Faye fell in love and were married. But as quickly as their signatures were on the marriage certificate, the marriage had problems. Regardless of the marital discord, Clayton Grissom was born November 30, 1978. He was a chubby-cheeked, adorable baby who never earned Vernon's affection or support. Vernon never contributed to Clay's life, regardless of his age. In fact, Grissom took exception to Clayton and reminded him, he was a mistake— not only in his comments but also in his indifference. Vernon drank excessively and he was physically abusive to Faye—he was later charged with assaulting his wife. Clay indicated he has seen pictures of the abuse.

Faye divorced Vernon Grissom when Clayton was three years old. *Rolling Stone* Magazine reports, "Clay Aiken and his father are estranged." Clay said, "He never tried to be a father to me, ever.... I saw him...growing up because the court made me.... My mom and Vernon got separated when I was one. We kind of lived on the run...we moved often to stay away from him." After the divorce however, Clayton was court appointed to have weekend visits with his alcoholic parent. For their father/son stopovers, Grissom would take young Clayton to the video store and get a handful of videos as Claytons designated weekend babysitter.

Vernon would then go out and leave Clayton alone or he'd

bring home a monochrome of barfly women or he would go to bed—he was often hung over. This was the weekend menu of toleration, VG offered his son. The time Clayton spent with his biological father is etched in Clay Aiken's memory. A reminder that a child's memory sponge soaks up family involvement, regardless of its contribution.

Clay has not seen nor spoken to his father since, who Aiken labeled his "sperm donor." Clay never refers to Grissom as his father—he calls him Vernon. Clay told Diane Sawyer during an interview on *Primetime* that their relationship was severed when he was 15 years old. He told his biological father he was the only one who initiated their visits and if Vernon wanted to see him to give him a call. Clayton said he would drive the ten-minute jaunt—just north of Raleigh so they could spend some time together. Vernon Grissom (in ten years) never called. Not once. Clay Aiken has risen above his father's neglect—many kids do not— many kids are damaged from slipshod parenting.

Faye Grissom was single for three years when her heart awakened. She and Ray Parker were both employed at Sears. Faye was an in-house Interior Designer; Ray worked in Home Improvements. They worked in close proximity, became friends and started dating. The match fit and they fell in love.... Faye Grissom wed Ray Parker in 1984. Faye had one son—6-year-old Clayton and Ray had two children, a 17-year-old boy Jeff and a 12-year-old daughter, Amy. Clayton was apprehensive about having a new dad, but Ray was a supportive father to Clayton. Ray and Faye Parker were strict but encouraging parents. The family grew up in a Southern Baptist environment and is steeped in deep religious principles.

Clayton was a bright and outgoing toddler. When he and his mother were in their car, his mother always had the radio tuned to a western station. The tot was only 18 months old when he started singing the country songs—his favorites were Kenny Rogers and Dolly Pardon's, "Islands In The Sun" and Willie Nelson's "Mommas Don't Let Your Babies Grow Up To

Be Cowboys."

When he was three, his mother often took him to Sears—her workplace. Faye's co-workers would put him on the carpet samples and bribe, "Clayton, we'll give you a dollar to sing." He would hesitate and pretend he was backward and shy and say, "I'm tired—I don't want to sing," because he knew the bribe would sometimes go up to $5.00. He would then back up to his mother and say, "Mom, wind me up." His mother would act like she was winding his tiny back like a "Jack-in-the-Box" and the adorable Jack would perform and then stuff his pockets full of money.

The young Clayton rarely socialized or played with other children because Faye and her son moved from place-to-place to conceal their whereabouts from Vernon. As a result Clayton Grissom interacted mainly with females, spending most of the time with his mother and her friends or his grandmothers—therefore, he was more sociable with adults.

When Faye married Ray Parker, Clayton inherited a new older brother and sister but there was a definite age and social gap. His stepbrother was 11 years older and his stepsister was six years older than their young sibling—as a result Clayton always stayed close to his mother.

Regardless, the young Grissom was not a spoiled child. When he was mouthy he got his mouth washed out with soap, and if he was disciplined he had to cut a switch from a branch and bring it in for the spanking. This did not happen often but Clayton was a precocious handful and he was sometimes sassy. This talented youngster did more than sass—he loved to enter-tain, so when the opportunities surfaced, his mother encouraged him to sing. When he was five there was a high school Winter Dance singing competition; Clayton competed and sang the No.1 hit, "Islands In The Stream." And he won. He said, "I remember being up there and everybody was laughing at me and I said, 'Mom, they're laughing at me,' and she said, 'No, they think you're cute.'"

When Billboard interviewed Clay he said, "I saw a...magazine that read, '12 LP's for the price of one.'" So the young Clayton Grissom placed his order. "My mom was furious with the company for allowing a seven-year-old to do that. But all I had to do was tape a penny to that little piece of cardboard and send it in." And the LP's arrived.... In spite of his youthful business sense, Clayton had a harrowing experience as young child that still holds him hostage with aqua phobic fears. His friends said he almost drowned. As a result of the trauma—he won't swim or go near large bodies of water.

Regardless, Clayton was not afraid of the stage. By age

Stough Elementary
Photo: Geoffrey Graybeal

seven, he was performing in Community Theater productions. Plus, his father Ray Parker's brother-in-law had a country band and they sometimes invited him to sing his favorite western songs. He also sang in the Raleigh Boys choir, but he always favored Christian and Country music. Clayton said, "My mom was never a stage mom, she just drove me to various things and if somebody needed help to fundraise, she'd work the ticket booth."

Frances Wilson—a family friend, remembers the first time she heard Clayton sing in Church. "He blew me away—this tiny little boy with red hair and wire-rimmed glasses and a bow tie — and that incredible voice." Amazingly, Clayton has never had any real musical training. He took piano for about four months—didn't like it and quit. He also took voice lessons for two months—didn't like it then quit. He was born with the gift of music.

Bonnie Wallace

CHAPTER THREE

I took á day to search for God,
And found Him not, But as I trod
By rocky ledge, through woods
Untamed,
Just where one scarlet lily flamed,
I saw His foot print in the sod.

Bliss Carman-Vestigia

CLAY'S MIDDLE SCHOOL—
A BOLD AND PRECOCIOUS KID
(6th-8th grade)

Daniels Middle School
Photo: Geoffrey Graybeal

Clayton Grissom was a lanky idiosyncrasy in middle school. As a result, Classmates often taunted him. When the ridicule would start he'd say, "Forget you," and he'd walk away. He said, "If you act intimidated, they're going to keep doing it." So he stood his ground with the school bullies. However, the taunting did not stop Clayton. His brain was always clicking. It didn't matter if he was in class or working on a school project, his mind was always somewhere else—he was usually thinking about his next conquest or planning his next wise-crack-attack. Alisha Puckett remembers Clayton as often sarcastic, often theatrical, and borderline annoying. His hair was always neat, never out of place. He had tons of freck-les and even some boyish zits and he always wore jackets.

Alisha said Clayton would break out singing—in the middle of conversations, lec-tures, projects, lunch, or for anybody who would listen—and they listened. He also loved performing at hospitals and for children and for the elderly. And in the early school Coral Concerts, Clayton stood out because he was the only boy singing with 40 other girls. But it was obvious he was having fun.

Grissom was a high-energy proactive kid and he was always involved in a myriad of School activities, but he was not the sports aficionado. Clayton tried to play different sports— including soccer, baseball and he was a regular at T-ball but he finally quit. His mother stopped encouraging him to play sports when she realized "he can't even run." He was never inclined athletically. Sports do not invite skinny awkward kids who have a hard time putting one foot in front of the other. As a result, that lack of personal approval became evident when his explod-ing fan base displayed signs of Clay worship and he qualified, "I can't believe that anybody even likes me."

What was amazing about Clayton Grissom even though his peer approval wasn't bridled—he loved to sing. His mother finally dismissed his lack of coordination on the playing field and said," Let's just let him sing. That's all he wants to do." Yes, Grissom had something that many of his peers envied—that voice.

His voice became an ace for adolescent acceptance when in eighth grade his chorale instructor and fellow students began to acknowledge his talent. Regardless of his quest for endorsement, young Grissom had a lot of resolve that drove him through the pubescent hurdles. He participated in a lot of school functions, many of which were self-initiated.

In Raleigh, the Elementary School, Middle School and High School are all interconnected, they are a multi school complex that are only separated by grade distinction. You go down one hall for Stough Elementary School (1st to 5th grade) and then down another hall to Leesville Middle School (6th to 8th grade) and down another corridor to the Leesville Road High School (9th to 12th grade). The separate buildings were all added at different junctures. The middle school was built first, the elementary school was added next, then the high school was

7th grade   Photo: Geoffrey Graybeal

finished last to complete the educational tripod. However, the first edition—the Leesville Middle School wasn't finished when Clayton started 6th grade, so he went to Daniels Middle School in 6th grade and went to Leesville Middle School in 7th and 8th grade. Grissom then started Leesville Road High School in 9th grade and graduated later from that high school at the end of his 12th year in 1997.

The Raleigh school's yearbooks were named after the Lion. Subsequently, the Elementary school's yearbook was named "The Cub." The Middle school's yearbook was called the "Leo." And the High School yearbook was the "Pride." When Clayton was in 7th grade he was copy editor and he did most of the work on the yearbook and he also initiated several extracurricular projects.

When Clayton advanced to 8th grade he was co-copy editor with his friend Geoffrey Graybeal for the yearbook, the "Leo." Again, he spearheaded the project by writing most of the copy, including headlines, photo captions and edited the work of three or four staff writers.

The young Grissom was career minded at a very early age—he was always testing the occupational waters. While most adolescent boys spent time parading in the halls making eyes at girls, Clayton also played the field—not with sports and not with girls but with career prospects. Plus, he was an A+ volunteer and if a desired program wasn't available, he often created it.

Leo Yearbook Staff
Photo: Geoffrey Graybeal

Clayton was also a PEPI (Physical Education Pupil Instructor)—an elective course normally offered to high schools in Wake County—a program where students could teach PE (an hour a day) to Elementary Students. Since Leesville Road High School wasn't finished the opportunity was offered to the Middle School 8th graders. So Clayton volunteered in 1992 and 1993. He taught Physical Education and assisted with PE lesson plans and other activities that were class related.

Grissom was one of two PEPI students who assisted PE teacher Sherry Davis. Classes were held in the "multipurpose

Leesville Middle School
Photo: Geoffrey Graybeal

room" which had a stage and a carpeted area with gym equipment, a balance beam, a variety of mats, and colored tape designs and painted squares on the carpet. The PE classes' also included gymnastic exercises and games like "four square," plus other physical activities. The anomaly is 12 and 13 year olds' were teaching the 6, 7, 8, and 9-year-old kids. However, Clayton loved clowning around with the elementary students, plus PEPI helped foster those nurturing feelings toward kids, then later "kids with special needs."

This proactive 8th grader also wanted to be a broadcast journalist. There wasn't a journalism program offered so Clayton helped organize and was involved with the production for the school's first TV (WLMS) newscast. TV and radio stations east of the Mississippi are required to use a "W" identifier for the station (WRAL, WTVD, WDNC, etc.) name while those west of the Mississippi use a K (KBBL etc). So to sound like a "real" TV station, WLMS was created—largely a

7th grade
Photo: Geoffrey Graybeal

student run newscast of Leesville Middle School (LMS). Clayton participated in every aspect of the program. He was a reporter, plus he wrote copy for the anchors and other reporters. Clayton was also the first TV anchor. He covered a segment on Physical Education Pupil Instructors (PEPI) including an interview with the PE teacher. He also shot several different locations including the front of the elementary school, the gym's auditorium and then he walked down the balance beam at the end of the program. Then a student was hit by a car on Leesville Road that year and died. The first newscast was dedicated to the student's honor. Clayton offered the music in the tribute that ran with the young boy's picture that was placed at the end of the broadcast.

8th grade   G. G.

With Grissom's interest in journalism, for the school's "Career Day" in February of 1993, Clayton and his sidekick Geoffrey Graybeal spent the day at "The News and Observer" offices on McDowell Street in downtown Raleigh. The duet was assigned primarily with veteran reporter Treva Jones and other political reporters. They also met Governor, Jim Hunt; Lieutenant Governor, Dennis Wicker; Secretary of State, Rufus Edmonton; and News and Observer, publisher Frank Daniels and many others. The collective experiences of tagging along with reporters and meeting many important politicos prompted Clayton to push for a teen voice in the newspaper. Grissom spoke with Editor Daniels about the possibility of several Raleigh teenagers writing a weekly teen column. Daniels liked the idea and gave them an editor's name to talk to about the proposal. Clayton placed nonstop calls every day for months to various editors to pitch the idea. The column never came to fruition until their sophomore year. "The News and Observer," then began to devote space to the teen voice— an online newspaper "Nando Next" in 1995.

Clayton sang in every choir from 6th to 12th grade. Elsie Norton was Grissom's choral director in the 8th grade and she directed the show "Good Vibrations" a song and dance group. Clayton was an important member of the choral class and production cast. The ensemble traveled, performed everywhere and did competitions. Norton said, "Clay was very dedicated. He was always there when I needed him." She continued, "If anyone was going to audition for a solo, if Clayton was auditioning, other students wouldn't audition because they knew he'd probably get the part. The Triangle native had a voice that stood out from the rest."

8th grade Show Choir
Photo: Geoffrey Grayheal

Grissom always exuded his passion for music. His rising souvenir talent with his comedic ability to ham-it-up created an endearing audience because from every performance he received "excellent" feedback consistently from the crowd. His natural presence on stage became his emporium for entertainment. In all of the group choir photos Clayton stands out in front—literally. Front and center. Elsie Norton believes Clay will go the distance because he not only has that incredible instrument, he is a fast study—he learns songs quickly and an audience does not intimidate him.

Cle Picket of News 14 Carolina, points out "Aiken's success has students all over Wake County wishing for their chance in the spotlight and to be taught by the teacher who taught the singer who could become the next *American Idol*." (How about the next American singing sensation?) Norton is currently the director of choral music at Southeast Raleigh High School. Ashleigh Hocutt said, "When I found out I was going to Southeast Raleigh High School, I was like 'Oh my (Gosh), I'm going to be taught by the same teacher as Clay Aiken, so I'm really thrilled that I could be a student of Ms. Norton.'"

Gaye Deamer

9th grade Show Choir
Photo: Geoffrey Graybeal

18

CHAPTER FOUR

I know that I've got big ears and a big forehead and that my
hair sticks up,
but I'm happy with myself.
I'm not necessarily trying to win a
beauty pageant here.

Clay Aiken

LEESVILLE ROAD HIGH SCHOOL
WILL NEVER BE THE SAME
(9TH-11TH Grade)

Clayton's transformation from Middle School to High
School was almost as significant as his transformation from his
American Idol audition—as the red-headed, jugged-eared,
freckled-faced, coke-bottled eye-glassed kid to American's
handsome heart throb. He appears to evolve from the aquatic
larvae of an amphibian to polliwog to frog, to later as America's
Prince of Pop.

Leesville Road High School
Photo: Geoffrey Graybeal

Regardless, Grissom still carried a hyper bespectacled demeanor in High School and he dressed to kill—uh, fashion was not his strong suit. But Clayton went from Middle School to High School to a well-liked goof He had unusual appeal and gained acceptance with his peers and became part of a popular group of friends. Leesville Road High School opened its doors for the first time in 1994 with no Senior class—only Freshmen, Sophomores and Juniors. The school was brand spanking new and during its first two years the school was forging an identity—as a result they were creating new clubs and organizations. During this genesis, Clayton wanted to form a Young Political Club. He found a Leesville history teacher who volunteered to be the advisor. They held their first meeting and Grissom recruited some interested students.

9th grade   G. G

The school advisors felt they needed to have a Young Opposite Political Party, as an issue of fairness. They could not find support for the Opposite Party so the Political Club was not created. Regardless, Clayton was very politically active. He followed political races, had group discussions and had his sights of one day running for office. In addition, Grissom participated in a countywide young Political Party Club comprised of students from area high schools throughout Wake County and he attended the assembly meetings where they collected signatures for petitions. He was always interested in state and county government affairs. (Clay

Aiken obviously felt some nostalgia, when after *American Idol* he stood before Washington's politicians as an advocate for Special Needs Children and also for other child-related foundations he supports.)

 Grissom's political drive however, was not his first love. His first love was singing and he always sought any opportunity that was musically related. In the 9th grade choir he was one of only three or four boys in the entire choir class. He was not shy in a room full of girls; he entertained them not only with music but also with his slapstick shenanigans.

When he was 15 years old he auditioned to be the lead singer in a Gospel quartet. Clayton had an exceptional tenor voice but the other singers in the quartet were in there 40's and 50's. Plus CG had always been the lead singer; so having to harmonize was out of his realm of experience. Also, because he was too young for a driver's license, his mother would have to drive him to two to three performances a week plus take him to a weekly practice. Mrs. Parker was willing to chauffeur him for a paying job. However, the quartet was not paid for performing, they occasionally received small stipends for gas and bus maintenance. In addition, the quartet required a huge time commitment, because they sang all over the state—mainly on Friday and Saturday nights. Clayton would have no free weekends, besides he needed a part time job. Therefore, the applicant did not fit the quartet's "needs and wants" and their "needs and wants" didn't fit Clayton's desire to sing.

Later, Clayton found a job that paid. Grissom was hired at the local Winn-Dixie supermarket. He did routine grocery store duties, unloaded grocery trucks, helped stock shelves, and he bagged groceries. When he turned 16 he started working at the YMCA.

This 16 year old had a traumatic experience that still affects him. He ran over his kitten accidentally and watched it die (accidentally Peta). It was so traumatic, he thought the spirit of the cat came out and haunted him. Since that quirky incident he's been afraid of cats. He favors dogs—even goats but not cats. Clay had a pet goat named Zoe that he took with him, like a pet dog. Wherever Clay went, Zoe went; wherever Zoe went, Clay went. They were seen all around town.

11th grade   G.G.

However, Clay always voiced his love of performing. He said, "Every time I would sing in a choir," I'd say, "This is what I want to do for the rest of my life." "Every time I'd do a play," I'd say, "This is what I want to do for the rest of my life." He loved the stage, but he usually needed a push to audition. His father Ray Parker always encouraged him. Clayton was his favorite singer. Mr. Parker heard of a competition in Johnston County. CG responded, "I don't want to go to Johnston County, they don't have anything down there." Finally, the 17-year-old Grissom ventured to the County auditions east of Riley and tried out. He won the local country singing contest and began performing in community shows.

11th grade Show Choir
Photo: Geoffrey Graybeal

The Daily Record in Dunn, NC and Ronnie Womack confirmed that he and Clayton Grissom became acquainted when they auditioned for a country music show at Smithfield's Johnston Community College. They both made the cut and each performed as soloists. The Dean was so impressed he recommended they get-together and sing. They took the advice and added two more singers to form a quartet, "Just By Chance." The crowds loved their country and gospel music. Later, the quartet left the College and they sang everywhere.

"Just By Chance," and its band had a close relationship.
Interestingly, Ronnie Womack said his first impression of
Clayton was, "How can that voice come from that body." A
statement later cloned by celebrity judge Lionel Richey.
Grissom's voice was heard all around the surrounding commu-
nities—Raleigh, Charlotte, Smithfield, Dunn, Lillington,
Clinton and other areas of Harnett and Johnston counties.

11th grade—goofing around
Photo: Geoffrey Graybeal

Mr. Womack said he is amazed at Clay's transformation.
(See "The Remarkable Transformation of Clay Holmes
Aiken.") "Clayton used to have long hair and glasses and his
maturity is what's so amazing." He said smiling, "I hardly recognized him." (One of my favorite quotes.) "He doesn't look
like the same person, but if you really look at the pictures you
can tell that is him in there."

Blends Created By Bonnie Wallace

Bonnie Wallace

CHAPTER FIVE

Let us then be up and doing,
With a heart for any fate;
Still achieving, still pursuing;
Learn to labor and to wait.

Longfellow-Psalm of Life

CLAYTON'S SENIOR YEAR IN HIGH SCHOOL
(EXHAUSTING!)

Evidence proves that Clayton Grissom was never a docile kid who sat in a muted corner. Keep in mind most of the students in his Senior class at Leesville Road High knew who he was. His inquisitive and loquacious natures on *American Idol* and on the post-Idol talk shows are the real Clay Holmes Aiken and his school involvement proves it. In the Senior Superlatives of the 1997 Edition of "Mycenaean," the Leesville Road High School newspaper, Clayton was tagged the "Gossip Mill." This busy boy had his fingers in everything and he kept the gossip and extra curricular staff on its toes. Then in another 1997 edition of "Mycenaean," siding with his friend's appraisal, CG was named "Most Sarcastic." Yes, look at the poles-apart personalities of Grissom because in the same year, the 1997 "Mycenaean," credits Clayton Grissom as the "Voice Of Pride." Pride is their school yearbook.

12th grade   G.G

The Raleigh teenager was always a self-starter but as mentioned, he usually displayed a playful wit coupled with a clear voice of sarcasm. He could fight back. His friends reported they were surprised at Clayton's composed demeanor as they watched him take the weekly beatings from the caustic *American Idol* judge Simon Cowell, because they said, "The Clayton Grissom we know would have come back with sharp retorts."

CA is not only sharp rhetorically; he was involved in most of the "comings and goings" of "everything that was anything." Clayton was often the innovator of the activities involving his membership. Clay said, "I was a B student and I hate to say this, but I never did homework but I managed to get good grades on tests." The kid is smart as a whip but it was obvious why he never did homework. He didn't have time. How could he possibly do homework, when he was the vanguard of every extra curriculum vitae from here to eternity, plus go to school? In addition, "Y" employee Mary Ann Lape, reported that he worked every day after school at the YMCA from 3 pm to 6pm.

The gazelle never slows down. When the other *American Idol* contestants were asked who was most competitive singer, they all undeniably said, "CLAY!". Simon Cowell said Clay was one of the most competitive people he has ever met.

As a result, his competitive nature ponders this question. "Does this guy ever sleep?" This sleepy question was asked of Clayton's friends. They responded, "Hardly." Aiken said since *American Idol* he has learned to get by on five hours sleep a night. Jerome—Clay's big handsome bodyguard said Clay is sometimes so exhausted he could sleep standing up.

12th grade Executive Council
Geoffrey Graybeal

This is obviously the norm because read on and see the EXTRA curricula's in the life of Clayton Grissom in just his Senior year in High School. Many wonder how this student ever found time to attend class. The school administrators said he had good attendance. One can see why this 6' 1" leggy male, only weighs 145 lbs. dripping wet—there's good reason. His motorized metabolism obviously has a hard time keeping up with his motorized schedule.

CG is not only a multi task person he is an organizer. However, there was one area of his person that was not organized—the way he dressed. Comfort was his only dress code. He was infamous for wearing reoccurring plaid shorts in high school—and color coordination was not on the agendas of this restless, unique kid. The Leesville Roads principal said, "Clayton was the only student in the entire school who wore a pair of bright yellow high-top sneakers." One could envision him coming down the hall with his crimson red hair, a high-buttoned striped shirt, two undershirts, those multi colored plaid shorts and those flashing yellow high top sneakers. "Here comes Clayton!" It was announced that Aiken loves "instant Grits," it was also well known Aiken loved "instant Garb." And no wonder he didn't date much, how could this energetic suspected insomniac, spare any time for rendezvous. He would have to take his girlfriend in those plaid shorts and high top yellow sneakers to Student Council—now that would have been a memorable date.... I'm "Sleepless In Salt Lake," just thinking about it. I'm also "Sleepless In Salt Lake" just cata-loguing the rest of this student's activities. Wait until you read the rest of his story....

Clayton's Senior Year Continued...
Leesville Road High School, Class of 1997
377 students were in Clayton's graduating class

Regardless of his standard of dress, this guy is amazing. Here are a few reminders of Clayton's Senior year at Leesville Road High in the town of Raleigh and the state of North Carolina....

Clayton was the Senior Class Representative to the Executive Council of student government; he was responsible to students and teachers in governing his Senior Class. He was also the Publicity Secretary in charge of the year-round publicity generated for the Graduates. He was also responsible for writing, then reading various morning school announcements over the P.A. system. Clayton also initiated and planned many events that took place throughout the school year such as the Homecoming Halftime Show and the Fall Pep Rally (which he co-emceed). In between his emceeing responsibilities that went on all year round, he assisted in the local food drives.

12th Student Government Council
Photo: Geoffrey Graybeal

Grissom also belonged to the 12th Grade Choir and partici-pated in all of the choir performances, often as the soloist. He was appointed to the court for the Winter Wonderland Dance—numerous Kings and Queens were nominated and the students voted for their favorite royal couple. Clayton sang "Unchained Melody," at the coronation of the "King and Queen." He announced over the PA system the winners of the homecoming royalty at the football game. He then sang at the end of the Wonderland assembly.

A side note—he also attended his required class schedule, plus as mentioned, he also worked after school at the YMCA from 3 pm to 6 pm. The teenager always sang at functions ad infinitum and he was not shy in changing his hair color, ad infinitum. His fire engine hair was sometimes highlighted to blondish red.

And his never-ending performances continue.... Grissom sang, "The National Anthem," before the Senior Night boys' basketball game. He also sang the "The National Anthem," numerous times before the now-defunct minor league hockey team, The Raleigh Ice Caps. A classmate said, "Clayton brought tears to English teacher Patsy Stone's eyes in 1997 when he sang 'My Girl,' to her on her birthday."

Then, Clayton brought the crowd to its feet at a packed Raleigh Memorial Auditorium when he sang "Pieces of Gold" at the annual arts showcase for Wake County schools' that showcases singers from high school choruses across the state....

And Clayton did date...he didn't have a steady girlfriend, but he and his buddies went on group dates. For the Senior Prom, he and 14 of his friends rented a bus and drove to Wrightsville Beach, a 2-1/2 hour drive from Raleigh. The entourage ate at the Oceanic Restaurant, took photos on the beach in their formal attire and drove back to the dance. Grissom's date was a girl from Texas.

Clay has pointed numerous times that his biological father was such a poor role model, he said, "I learned to be who I am by being everything that he wasn't."

Clay doesn't drink—Vernon was an alcoholic.

Clay is not a racist—Vernon was a racist.

Clay is not a womanizer—Vernon was a womanizer.

Clay doesn't curse—Vernon cursed. Subsequently, Clay reprimands anyone who curses.

Clay does not participate in wild partying. (Vernon Grissom passed away February 2004 at the age of 68 of heart failure.)

Because Clay does not drink, he was always the designated driver for parties.

Vernon Grissom didn't realize what an opposite affect he would have on his son—for good.

A fact that is not good—Clayton has a mountain of allergies. He's allergic to mint, chocolate, coffee, shellfish, mushrooms, almonds and other tree nuts. He especially has a dramatic reaction to mint, coffee and chocolate. Clay said in an interview, 'When these are eaten by mistake he says it feels like his chest is convulsing. It's like giving birth out of my chest." He also displayed some other health concerns in High School. He had an inner ear imbalance that was so severe he couldn't walk. He came to school for a couple of days in a wheel chair.

Grissom also suffered from hypoglycemia. A friend remembers when he had a seizure at School. He needed help and asked for a Mountain Dew. The students ran and coined a can of the pop from the vending machine and ran back and put the unopened can on his desk. A scene was created watching him struggle to peel the can open while he was in a state of dangerously low blood sugar. Hypoglycemic people can have a reaction if they skip meals or are unusually active. Clay indicated he usually only eats one meal a day.

Memorial Auditorium
Photo Geoffrey Graybeal

Clayton was involved in endless theatrical and/or musical productions.

Dates, not chronicled.) Including performances at the North Carolina Theatre in:

— "1776" with Terrance Mann, a renowned North Carolina actor.

—He also performed in "Shenandoah."

—Clayton acted in "Sound Of Music" with Frankie Muniz.

—Clay was in "Cinderella" at Raleigh Little Theatre for three years.

—He also was the host of "The Hometown Music Connection," a bi-monthly concert variety show in Benson.

—Joan Mclendon verified he also performed "The Wizard of Opry, at   the Johnston Community College Country Music Showcase.

A family friend, Francine Wilson sometimes performed With Clayton, posing as his "Aunt Francine." He would devise comedy routines, such as having "Francine" dive face-first into a chocolate cake. That was typical Clayton.

The young Grissom also sang regularly in the YMCA staff meetings, with the YMCA's youth performances and in the Leesville Baptist church he attended in North Raleigh. He also entertained the crowds at beauty pageants. (Obviously, the Miss America Pageant was not his first.) Clayton entertained in hospitals, old folk homes, various schools, and he has sung at a surfeit banquet of weddings and funerals and you-name-its-there are so many, he says he's lost count.

Photo: Geoffrey Graybeal

Then Adam Barbour said he performed with Clayton for eight years, long enough to see him miss a few notes and to realize he had potential star power. Barbour continued, "He could always work a crowd...but I knew he'd be a famous...singer some day."

Clayton Grissom graduated from Leesville Road High School in 1997.

Blends Created By Bonnie Wallace

CHAPTER SIX

Clay's creativity and ability to motivate others was evident
as a student and these traits shine through on stage.

—Clay Aiken's Professor, Cheryl Young

AFTER HIGH SCHOOL—COLLEGE—
TO HIS AMERICAN IDOL AUDITION

Clayton was accepted to a music conservatory to further his
musical studies once he graduated from high school, but he
declined. He felt there was no security or future as a singer. His
mother encouraged him to wait before going to college full time
for a break to decide what he wanted to pursue.

Clayton was hired as a substitute teacher in the Wake
County schools. He worked in an elementary autism classroom
in Raleigh for two years while going to college part time at a
local community college. Plus, he worked at the YMCA also
working with some dysfunctional students. Those collective
teaching experiences formulated what he wanted as a career

because he loved working with challenged kids. Some kids are not coupled with the proper chemistry conductors required for motorized and/or verbal communique . As a result, Aiken says he's been spit on and kicked—he's been punched, and he says he's even been peed on because autistic people will try anything to communicate with you. However, Clay relished in helping them try to put the pieces of this puzzle in a workable frame. He said their challenge became his challenge.

North Carolina University
Photo: Geoffrey Graybeal

UNC Charlotte
Photo: Geoffrey Graybeal

In North Carolina there are 16 public Universities that are part of the UNC system. The University of North Carolina at Chapel Hill is the only one that "UNC" is an acceptable second reference. If people refer to UNC they are talking about Chapel Hill—it is the nation's oldest public university. All of the other UNC campuses have their city attached as the second reference. For example, The University of North Carolina at Charlotte would be UNC Charlotte or UNCC.

Once Clayton found his niche, he went to UNC Charlotte to complete the last two years for his degree in Special Education. When he entered the university, he was no longer a Grissom; he enrolled as "Clayton Aiken." He had mentally, emotionally and legally erased his biological father from his life by shifting his last name to his mother's genealogy of Aiken. The theorem of change was in admiration of his supportive maternal caretaker and to honor that ancestry line of her stewardship.

What did not change was the love and respect Clay gleaned from the UNCC faculty and his associates.... Professor Nancy Cooke indicated that Clay was President of UNCC's Student Chapter Of The Council For Exceptional Children plus he tutored several autistic children.... Aiken's professor Cheryl Young added, "Clay's creativity and ability to motivate others was evident as a student, and these traits shine through on stage." Wendy Wood, his faculty advisor, also has high accolades for the university student, plus she didn't fault young people for following their dreams—she added, "I also love the way he looks." Alisha Puckett, the editor-in-chief of UNCC's campus newspaper said that two months before Clay auditioned for *American Idol*, he called begging her for a reporter to cover a charity dance he was organizing to benefit disabled senior citizens.

The Shinn family—mother Michelle "Mimi," and her daughters give glowing reports of Aiken—he tutored their autistic son and brother, Nicolas. Clay worked with the young boy six hours a day several days a week, for almost a year in 2000 and 2001. Nicolas struggles from a disability known as Fragile X syndrome. Charlotte Observer, Staff writer Leigh Dyer wrote, "Nicolas suffers with attention deficits, mental retardation and problems with his nervous system." He doesn't recognize certain sensations and sounds... "For example, he can burn himself...because he doesn't recognize when things are hot....

"His charm showed through from the first time he knocked on their door." Mimi Shinn continued, "There is something about Clayton—he just walks into a room and fills up the room.... He is like a family member. He's definitely the kind of person you can always count on." Aiken was patient but firm with Nicolas. He taught him do basic things to function.

Clay loves working with special needs kids. He said,

"When you work with kids who have autism, they don't reciprocate any affection. You learn to find your self-worth within what you do, not what people tell you about yourself."

No one questioned Aiken's abilities, but his hair challenged approval—the styles and colors changed with the semesters. His figurine mahogany hair was often rolled around perm rods then dipped in peroxide. Clay grimaced when he saw the blond curls revealed (on a huge screen) when he appeared on the Oprah show. His fans giggled with approval.

And others also offer their approval. Aiken said he went with a girl in college and the relationship lasted a few months. However, he countered he's never had his heart broken because he's never been in love. Erik Hedegaard asked Clay if he's ever broken anyone's heart. "I don't think so," he says, "I mean, come on, hello! The way I see it, I'm not that big of a prize." Tell that to those "Aiken fans" they have a different story.

However, while Clay was attending UNC Charlotte and coaching autistic teens, there was a shocking concern on the biological Grissom front. Clay wasn't aware that his half sister Debra was suicidal. Vernon Grissom always favored his daughter, but had notably turned his back on his male progeny. When Clay made the legal transfer of his last name from Grissom to Aiken, Debra called him to express her disbelief. Aiken didn't want the confrontation so he never returned her call. The following February his mother telephoned him at the University and told him that Debra had died—from a self-inflicted gunshot wound. Clay was devastated and it took a long time for him to stop blaming himself for her death.

Regardless, bereavement does not always cave family syllogism.... Months later when Clay Aiken had become a household name, Clay's grandmother Grissom died and Aiken attended the funeral. The family told the funeral director to ask the "famous attendee" to leave.... Vernon Grissom had talked to the tabloids and they had printed misleading stories about his mother. When Aiken was interviewed on national television and in magazines, he defended his mother and himself by telling the real story of his biological father and exposed that he had never participated in his life and called him his "sperm donor." And he also announced that Ray Parker was the only father he had ever known. (Clay did not attend Vernon Grissom's funeral when he passed away in February 2004.)

Aiken came home at the end of spring semester and worked at the YMCA summer camps. (One report said he also waited on tables—no dates indicated.) In the fall he returned to UNCC to resume his studies. At that time he was placed with another autistic boy Mike Bubel (Mike Jr.), and worked with him during that year. Diane Bubel, Mike Sr. and their daughter Emma had rave reviews for Clayton—not only referring to the work he did with Mike Jr. but he was like family. They said, "He sang, he always sang." The Bubels were not only enthralled with his voice, they have deep affection for their favorite tutor.

Clay returned home for the summer, and again worked at the seasonal camps at the YMCA. However, this summer his father Ray Parker was hospitalized and died unexpectedly from pulmonary fibrosis on July 4, 2002. Clay again worked at the YMCA then spent time at the bedside of his dying father. The family then had to deal with the grief and aftermath of Ray Parker's sudden death. With the traumatic summer behind him Aiken returned again to UNC Charlotte to finish his degree and to continue tutoring Mike. The Bubel family loved Clay's singing and they thought he should further a music career. He loved performing but he had been-there, done-that-he had per- formed most of his life.... Diane said he should audition for *American Idol*. Aiken said, "No!" In fact he wanted to try out for the *Amazing Race*. He and a female friend were ready to hand in their entrance papers. He also had someone as a backup in case they wouldn't accept his feminine partner. The Bubels kept pushing *American Idol*. Clay kept saying, "No! He wanted to try for *Amazing Race*. Finally, Diane and Emma would not take no for an answer, plus *American Idol* auditions were being held in Charlotte. Because of their constant badgering, Clay finally said he would audition if they would "Keep Quiet! And Quit nagging him!"

Aiken tried out in Charlotte and was cut. The challenge began. He learned they had new auditions in Atlanta. Aiken called his mother and told her he was driving to Atlanta. His family was very supportive. They needed a diversion after the tragic loss of their husband and father. Clay's mom and their family were happy to have something to rally behind. Faye said, "God closes doors, and he opens other ones."

Note.... Clay continued his University studies after *American Idol* and graduated from UNCC on December 20, 2003 with a degree in Special Education—he is still required to complete a semester of Student Teaching to receive his teaching certificate. But his school teaching days have most assuredly taken a slight detour.

YCMA—A.E. Finley main building
Photo: Geoffrey Graybeal

CHAPTER SEVEN

Nicknames were a tradition at the YMCA. The students attached several names to Clay. One of his first nicknames was "Paperboy" because he always had papers in his hands. Another nickname was "Carrot Top" because of his bright red hair. Then Clay was renamed, "Wonder bread" because this wonder boy was told his skin was white like bread and his hair was the color of crust. The final nickname that stuck is "Gonzo."

Clay and YMCA Staff

THE YMCA AND CLAY

The YMCA was a positive, synergistic experience for Clayton Grissom, alias Clay Aiken. He was involved in the Young Men's Christian Association most of his life.

There are more than 2,400 YMCA's (Y's) serving 10,000 communities in the United States, and each community offers different programs and events. In addition, the YMCA's arms stretch beyond the United States and they are working in more than 120 countries around the world, serving more than 30 million people—the largest, non-profit community service in the United States. The "Y" is for people of all faiths, races, abilities, ages and incomes. No one is turned away for inability to pay. The YMCA Mission is: "To put Christian principles into practice through programs that build healthy spirit, mind and body, for all."

Clay said in a CNN interview, "My passion for teaching came out of one of those phases where I was tired of being known as the singer, so a friend of mine convinced me to come and work with her at the "Y" just one evening a week.... I loved it so much, I decided to do the summer camp program." Clayton was later, an after-school Youth Counselor, weekdays from 3 p.m. to 6 p.m. As indicated, he was also employed for their summer's camps from 7:30 am to 6 pm, including his summer breaks while attending UNC Charlotte. Grissom worked at the YMCA for eight years—until he auditioned for *American Idol*.

The students were on a "tracking program." They attended nine weeks of regular school, they had three weeks off and this rotated all year round. So the YMCA classes would fill up consistently as the on-going tracking groups would rotate into the "Y's" curriculum. As a result, they were never without kids to tutor. The classes were structured but the counselors were able to interject their individual personalities in the calendar of events and Clayton's hilarious and eclectic antics kept everybody laughing and on their toes. Grissom also attended bimonthly family nights with parents and their children, plus he participated in regular staff meetings. The counselors worked as a team and they were in charge of approximately nine children each.

Amazingly, Clayton worked this YMCA schedule sandwiched in between his High School classes and extra curricular activities and in the middle of all of his musical performances. This seems almost impossible if you look at his High School involvement alone. He also worked at the "Y" for five to six years after graduation when he was a substitute teacher, also going to college part time and again in between all his singing engagements. (A YMCA employee said she questioned if he ever slept.)

Grissom sometimes worked the front desk and did anything that was required of him. Regardless, everybody at the "Y" was an enthusiast of Clayton Grissom Aiken. Jeff Flake, a YMCA supervisor of after-school programs, told the News & Observer, "I have witnessed him take a child with autism who couldn't communicate, and by the end of the school year, with Clayton just talking to her and working with her with cue cards and picture cards, that child could say a handful of words."

The counselors who worked with him are some of his best friends and they have deep affection for each other. Clay said he wished he had the talent of one of his partners Meridith Cox, because "even her handwriting is art." Meridith expressed admiration for Aiken. She said, "Not only does he have star quality, he's witty with a sarcastic sense of humor. He was willing to do whatever it takes to get the job done: put on a (costumed) dress, do different accents, whatever is necessary to get the campers laughing." Another counselor added, "He loved sports, games, and just having fun. He was one of those good-natured counselors. The only bad part was, he was kinda moody. But that just shows that he is just a regular old guy." *Old guys, did you hear that?* Another employee said, "He was usually happy and laughing." Then a Clay admirer chimed in, "His unique and crazy personality endeared Clayton to everyone. He has had a positive influence on hundreds upon hundreds of children who affectionately nicknamed their beloved head counselor, 'Gonzo.'"

The delightful Mary Ann Lape who has worked at the YMCA for over 13 years knows Clayton Grissom Aiken well. She said laughing, "He was a piece of work!" She continued laughing and she laughed so hard talking about the YMCA's favorite employee we both began guffawing and the interview resulted in pages of zigzagged notes.

Mary Ann worked at the front desk. She said. "I can still see him coming through that door—and you never knew what was coming when he came through that door. He was such a character." And he was always asking for things. "I need this!" and "I need that!" (Clay's mother Faye, said every time he calls her he says, "Mom, I need you to do this" and "I need you to do that." The long and the short of this story is—this superman needs a personal "gopher-to-get-this and a gopher-to-get-that." However, it's obvious he might have some additional help since becoming El Numero on Planet Clay. Forging ahead, a YMCA employee was asked, "How did he dress?" She paused— "Dress?" She continued, "He always wore plaid shorts—one whole summer he wore plaid shorts." Those plaid shorts are infamous because Grissom's high school principal said, "Clay always wore these plaid shorts."

Regardless, Kristy Hall, Clay's supervisor remembers distinctly when Clayton let the kids' duct tape him to the wall. When the taping was about to begin, he asked Mary Ann if she could find some gym pants so the tape wouldn't stick to the hair on his legs. I don't think they found any leggings so when he was de-stripped of tape his legs might have been de-stripped of hair. At any rate, the end results turned him into a caricature of solidly silver Clay.

Lape said Clayton reminded her of Jim Neighbors. He was like the character Jim Neighbors played on the Andy Griffith show—then she stopped and said quietly, "When he sang, it was magic." He always performed with the YMCA students and he sang regularly at staff meetings.

Mary Ann was asked to describe Clay Aiken in one word. She immediately responded, "Flamboyant!" She then paused and said, "Humble." She continued, "He knows when to lay on the fun, but he knows when to turn it off."

This author asked if she was surprised to see the demure gentleman Clay Aiken, on *American Idol*. She said, "Oh Heavens No! That's Clay! That's just how he is." She added, "He can be clowning around one minute, but when he stands up to perform he's not the same person—with the audience there is a reverence, and then there's a meltdown." Lape paused, "Just before he left to go to California, he sang a couple of songs at our staff meeting and it's hard to explain how we felt." She continued, "The YMCA has an annual, 'We Build People,' campaign. Clayton wrote and sang an original song for the Victory Celebration. As he sang, hearts began to dissolve and by the time he was finished singing, there was not a dry eye in the audience."

I was about to hang up the interview when Mary Ann Lape interjected, "I want to tell you when Clay said, 'It's important that I make a difference,' he really meant it. And when he said he could quit and he would really be okay," she said, "He meant that too."

Clay told the News & Observer. "I enjoy singing, and I love performing. There's definitely a thrill you get from performing on stage when everybody's cheering for you, and then there's a completely different kind of thrill when you're working with children. You don't necessarily get the applause... the cheers... the pats on the back... but there's a different kind of acceptance...when you work with kids."

Clay has expressed his deep appreciation with the support the "Y" has given him with his experience from *American Idol*.

Gaye Deamer

CHAPTER EIGHT

Clay—I just don't see you as what we're looking for...
a recording artist

Simon Cowell

THE FABULOUS FOURSOME

By 2003, Reality TV proved it had captured an imposing audience with the major of networks. Consequently, *American Idol* could not be ignored because the show's commanding viewer ship garnered undeniable clout for the Fox Network. AI's platform created by Simon Fuller's 19 Entertainment: Discover fresh new talent; the contestants compete on national television. Their performances are critiqued by a panel of judges; then the viewing audiences vote for their favorites. The winner is showcased as the next new Pop Star. The idea was brilliant and it has taken the country by storm. To find the next new Pop Star, *American Idol* holds auditions in selected cities around the country (each year approximately 70,000 hopefuls line the streets for their chance at fame). Corporate, plus a panel of judges slice the contenders down to a couple of hundred who are chosen to go to Hollywood. The Hollywood candidates continue the competition and are cut to 32—from those, the top 12 finalists are chosen. To get to the final 12 is a chance of a lifetime, because those contestants get to perform on the blockbuster television show *American Idol*, showcasing their talent before 25 to 30 million people—in addition, they are competing for a million dollar recording contract. *American Idol* is televised twice-a-week on the Fox Network with three renowned judges, plus new weekly celebrity guest judges, who critique their performances. The contestants perform the first night—after the show, the viewers cast their votes (calling toll-free numbers) for their top picks. The following night, one contestant with the fewest number of votes (with a lot of drama and fanfare) is eliminated. This format continues until the end of May until the public has (allegedly) chosen their *American Idol*.

However, the contestants are not the only reason viewers stayed tuned to their televisions on Tuesdays and Wednesday nights. There are four cornerstones—a compelling mix of personalities who shore-up the show's success.

The Fabulous Foursome—the three judges of *American Idol*—Randy Jackson, Paula Abdul and Simon Cowell and the host, Ryan Seacrest. Their credentials bedazzle the entertainment industry. And they each add the charismatic persona that makes the show so successful:

RANDY JACKSON

The first chair of the judging trio is Randy Jackson. Mr. Jackson's track record is so imposing, this giant has immense clout in the music industry. Yes, "This Dawg is top Dawg!"

Randy Jackson's expertise comes from hands on experience—a thesaurus in apprenticeship. He knows the business. His twenty-years as an industry veteran honored him with a Grammy as an Award winning producer. He was Vice President of A&R at Columbia Records for eight years, then Senior Vice

President of A&R at MCA Records for four additional years. Randy Jackson has been instrumental in creating over one thousand gold and multi-platinum albums with sales of over 200 million worldwide.

Jackson has tutored, recorded and/or toured with: Clay Aiken, Mariah Carey, Celine Deon, Whitney Houston, NSYNC, Madonna, Elton John, Destiny's Child and many more.

The *American Idol* contestants and audience appreciate Jackson's forthright critiques. They trust his politic guidance because he has tutored the elite.... Music is his life, but so is his family—a gorgeous wife—a former ballet dancer and three adorable daughters. Some men fake fatherhood, but Randy Jackson even with his breakneck schedule stays true to family values.

American Idol's stage of show-and-tell with Jackson's euphonious eye is an automatic sifting machine of separating the chaff from the wheat. However, Jackson used to be a kinder critic but now he doesn't waste any praise. He's giving Simon a run for his mouth.

Fox with *19 Entertainment,* writes about Randy Jackson. "With his amazing talent, immense studio knowledge, performing, touring and record company experience, Randy is one of today's most highly coveted music industry experts." The viewing audience qualifies they are proud to have Mr. Randy Jackson, sitting in the judge's chair.

PAULA ABDUL

Ruben Studdard said, "Paula Abdul is one of the nicest people you would ever want to meet." Ruben said o*n Live With Regis and Kelly,* that Paula is the mother figure. "She's like the mother of the judges." Kelly Ripa (the most feisty and spirited blond on television) really played on the Ruben /Paula mother snafu. She yelled, "You heard it here Paula! Ruben called you his mother!" Ruben, "I don't mean Mother." Kelly, "Sure you did!" Ruben recanted "Paula, you know I love you baby!" All the contestants and the worldwide audience also "love you baby!"

Paul Abdul is no stranger to success. Her life's dream was to be a dancer. She took dance lessons from the age of nine and with her natural gift for acting, at age sixteen, Abdul landed the role in the 1978 movie—musical "*Junior High School*." She became a Cheerleader for the *LA Lakers* and because of her ingenuous and dynamic dance style she was hired as the choreographer. Paula revolutionized Cheerleading within the industry.

However, it was while she was choreographing the *L.A. Lakers* that she was being watched by the Jackson Five As a result, she was hired by Janet Jackson to choreograph her smash hit video *"Nasty."* Abdul has worked on numerous films, plus she has also worked with entertainers—George Michael, Debbie Gibson, Duran Duran, INXS and ZZ Top.

When Simon Cowell was asked what artist he admired and respected the most— without hesitation he said, "Paula Abdul," and with good reason. Her astonishing career is coveted by worldwide album sales exceeding 30 million records, two (2) #1 Albums, six (6) #1 Singles, a *Grammy Award*, seven (7) *MTV Awards*, two (2) *Emmy Awards*, two (2) *People's Choice Awards,* and two (2) *Kids Choice Awards*. This tiny fireball has also been honored with her personal Star on Hollywood Boulevard and she was inducted in *Nickelodeon's Kid's Choice Hall of Fame*. It's remarkable what this woman has achieved in her impressive career.

Paula Abdul is a mother figure—she is the caretaker of the kids. The contestants fold safely under her wings. Without her, the judging trio would not be the same. She offers softer appraisal that cushions the harsher critics and she gives constructive criticism when it is needed. She encouraged Clay Aiken to dance and he upped his tempo with Buttercup'd dancing and it worked —especially for the Clay fans. She gives standup applause when it is deserved and she just makes everyone feel better. She raises Simon's eyebrows, especially with her diamond and ice-skating comparisons but Simon's eyebrows rarely sit still. Most importantly she is Paula Abdul—and need we say more?

SIMON COWELL

Simon Cowell, the British *BMG Records* Executive exhibits an impressive track record. Cowell has a music career of over 20 years and is considered to have influenced pop music as it is today. He has sold over 95 million albums, over 100 top 30 records and 40 #1 singles. Westlife; also the pop sensation, Sinatta; and Robson and Jerome are artists he has helped develop prior to his *American Idol* fame.

Simon Cowell is not only a man of accomplishment; he is a man of interest—to say the least. He is the man you hate to love, but he is the attention-getter with his infamous put-downs on *American Idol*. He cut a swath through the UK with the trendy show *Pop Idol*, with his bodyguards having to protect his every strut. Cowell divulged that he left some UK kids with such revenge for smashing their dreams; they warned they were out to get him. He admitted, some threatened him with baseball bats. He needs bodyguards to protect his yap because if gravity prevents him from flapping those lips, he could be out of work. (It has since been reported that he has insured his mouth for one-and-a-half million.) Smart boy.

Simon thundered on U.S. soil and took over the American Air Waves as one of the creators, then as the acrid-tongued judge of *American Idol*. Simon Cowell is a Marketing Genius of self-promotion. He markets his own sarcastic appeal with self-centered ego. Cowell knows how to market Cowell; and we all watched as he nozzled our attention with his calculated celebrity. *American Idol*'s obsession has grown to such dominance that 33 million viewers tuned in for the finale 2003 show. Competitors scramble to compete with this blockbuster—a talented expose with the sundry of judges and the sharp young host Ryan Seacrest, who stands up boldly to Simon's baboonery. Simon Cowell however, is the potentate of AI fascination with his caustic show-stopping antics.

Some people are entertained. Some are not. Mr. Cowell has acquired some labels—many argue he is America's most hated Brit. Others compared him to the biting, hard-edged Brit, Ann Robinson from the *Weakest Link*. Others renamed him, "Osimon Bin Laden," while others call him "Cowbell" or "Slimon." On the other hand, many viewers feel he is the most straightforward judge and gives the most clear-cut critiques.

Regardless, the *American Idol* audience keeps growing and they stay tuned to the Tuesday and Wednesday night Fox program. Many of the viewers wait for the Simon SLAMs— and they get what they tuned in for—that unstoppable mouth. That mouth has earned him amazing notoriety. The ageless, Regis Philbin on *"Live with Regis and Kelly,"* said "Simon Cowell was one of the most talked about figures in the entertainment business." Regardless of his fame, Fox Producers warned him to tone down his brutality. He ignored the warnings as he continued to cut-up contestants like paper dolls and berated "the Fox" on National Television.

Simon became an overnight "pain in the ask-me-no-questions and I'll tell you no lies." He lies admittedly about some contestant's performances that he does not want to win. As a result, when his acrimonious jowl repeatedly attacked Clay Aiken, the battering also pierced the audience and they countered and booed his cruel assaults so loudly you could not hear him speak. To get his comments heard above the angry crowd, Simon turned and yelled at the audience, "WILL YOU SHUT UP?"

However, Simon Cowell's appeal is not always shut up! He has an entourage of women who are bewitched by him, including Paula Abdul. But he is equally smitten with the diminutive beauty. Randy Jackson on *Oprah* laughed, with tongue-in-cheek and said "There is so much love and tension between them!" That depends on what day of the week it is because they often claim disdain for each other. Regardless, Simon hurls digs at Paula and the rest of the world without smiling.

Possibly the reason Simon doesn't smile, he is always nego-tiating. Negotiators seldom smile. With regard to *American Idol* 3, he indicated he might leave the show. Cowell announced on a zillion T.V. Talk and Entertainment shows, "I've got other things to do." And in the Los Angeles Times he reported, "The show is a six-month commitment, and (coming back) will depend on whether we can make the right deal. Right now, it's up in the air." (The air started thickening.)

Cowell received incredible exposure on the U.S. airways. The Brit expose' *Pop Idol* doesn't hold a candle to the U, S of A-land of opportunity. In an interview with *Times*, Cowell indi-cated the best thing about the exposure afforded by the show (*American Idol*) is that network execs now take him seriously.

And seriously they do—another Network plus Fox bet big bucks on this Hit Man. CBS signed his controversial pen at match making, the Reality Television Program, *Cupid* in which Cowell co-produced under Cupid Productions, Inc. He says the *Cupid* show did not have the same biting criticism as AI. Well possibly, but the show did have criticisms.... One CBS affiliate refused to air the show; charging that *Cupid* was "demeaning to marriage." Another reality check—*Cupid* had very mediocre ratings.

Regardless, Simon ignored the criticisms. *Cupid* was aired on another network—not with Fox and Cowell announced his possible departure from *American Idol*, which is the music world's hottest Franchise. Then when Fox Network's *American Juniors* show drew a paltry 8.4 million viewers compared to *American Idol*'s 2003 average of 21.8 million viewers, Simon was leveraged to his kilt.

The Fox caved in. Simon got exactly what he wanted and announced he is "absolutely thrilled" with the pact. Fox execu-tive Sandy Grushow said, (with a crooked smile), "Simon Cowell has a unique voice and point of view that obviously res-onates all over America. That means we'll have to put up with him for years to come."

THE REPORTED DEAL: Cowell committed for three more years as The *American Idol* Judge—good until 2006. (He wasn't committed—the report said, he committed.) Watch out wannabe's "Here comes Cruel!" Also, Fox would assist in setting up Simon Cowell's new production company, Simcow, ltd. Fox will get "first choice" options on the next three new shows from Sincow ltd. "Within the next 48 months, I fully expect to have two or three shows on the air. Definitely!" SC told the Times. The reports indicated   Simon was paid 45 million for three more Idol years —hundreds of thousands per SLAM. Not bad for the judge who said Idol was boring. The hundreds of thousands per Slam, takes the B and the O and the R and the I and the N and the G right out of his vocabulary. But don't count on it. His middle name is controversy.

When Simon Cowell's three-year contract was announced over the International Airways there were cheers and jeers. Supporters claim *American Idol* would not be the same without him. His detractors' claim the show would be better off without the psychological battering he inflicts on contestants.   The popular show with Simon Cowell is telling the tale.

RYAN SEACREST

Ryan Seacrest said on *Entertainment Tonight*, "being chosen to be the host of *American Idol* has been a dream come true." What a dream! However, the dream could have turned into a sleepwalk for the 29 year old charismatic host had he not pulled it off. But he pulled it off big time. The exposure for Seacrest has been phenomenal and he has secured himself as an important asset to the show.

The young host's engaging personality fits the genre of *American Idol* like a glove. He dodges Simon's bullets without bullet-proof-protection and returns the gunfire jibes with crack shot accuracy. Plus he keeps the show moving and on a high-energy track.

Ryan's interest in broadcasting peaked at a young age when he was selected to recite the Pledge of Allegiance over his

Dunwoody's high school's PA system. That recital set the wheels turning for a very promising career. At 16 years of age, he applied for an internship at one of Atlanta, Georgia's top radio stations, *WSTR/STAR 94 FM*. He was turned down. Ignoring the rejection, this persistent teenager submitted a demo tape to the director of programming and they could not ignore this energetic kid, plus they were impressed with his style. So, while Ryan was still a high school student he was offered the job as the on-air personality and eventually landed the 7 p.m. to Midnight gig. The show became one of the stations highest rated shows. He not only hosted the show he kept up his schoolwork and he also carved out time to play on his high school football team—he'll always be a Falcon fan.

Seacrest graduated from Dunwoody High School and attended the University of Georgia while still working at his popular show at *Star 94*. During his freshman year at the University, *ESPN* offered Ryan his first TV weekend show, hosting the daily sports game *"Radical Outdoor Challenge."* He became the game show anchor while still continuing his Georgia studies. Ryan then moved to LA in 1995 to test his prowess in the entertainment industry. He was hosting the LA afternoon local radio station *Star 98.7* when he learned of the search for the "host" of *American Idol*. He auditioned before the board of AI decision-makers and almost immediately, they said, "You've got the job." In addition to *American Idol* and *Star 98.7* he has worked *Ultimate Revenge*, on TNN. He also landed his own Fox Daily Talk Show, *On Air with Ryan Seacrest*. It was signed sealed and delivered in early 2004. Also, in the first quarter of 2004 he replaced Casey Kasem as host of *Radio's Top 40*. Wow! This savvy host of *American Idol* obviously does not waste his time.

Ryan Seacrest has most assuredly found his niche. He is praised and his accolades are everywhere. Most talk critics give him glowing reviews. This Mr. Macho Man was honored in the 2003 issue of *PEOPLE MAGAINE'S*, "50 MOST BEAUTIFUL PEOPLE." E! Online, has included Seacrest on their "Top 20 under 30 list reserved for twenty something Celebrities that have the most power in Hollywood."

This has all happened because a young kid gave the Pledge of Allegiance over the High School microphone and knew that it felt good.

Good for you guy! And good for *American Idol*—for giving us Ryan Seacrest.

Bonnie Wallace

CHAPTER NINE

"Mother! Are you all right?"
They seriously questioned if I were going
through a Mid-Life-Crisis....

A PARADIGM SHIFT IN BEHAVIOR

Reality TV has become a hook for many viewers. As a result, *American Idol* 2 became folly and fun for the world and me. Millions of us took a break from demanding work schedules and tuned-in Tuesday and Wednesday nights rooting for our favorites. *American Idol* caught my attention last year. I watched sporadically and wanted Kelly Clarkston to win but I never voted.

This year was different. Carmen Rasmussen was from my home state and the media was caught-up with her celebrity. I watched and voted for her (and another favorite). She was the palpable choice of Simon Cowell, who deemed her the most marketable of the contestants. In addition, Carmen was at the top of Internet polls as the young men's choice for their personal fantasies—the girl they dreamed about—the girl they would like to date. Clay Aiken said, "All the guys on the show had a crush on Carmen." Rasmussen climbed to the top six out of 70,000 American Idols entries—impressive for a young high school girl—she was only 17 when she entered the competition.

Then later, a fan of Carmen Rasmussen created some amusing entertainment during the *American Idol* Concert. This young man sat in front of me. On the contrary, he didn't sit. He went absolutely berserk every time she entered the stage. He would jump up and down, wave his arms wildly and give megaphone yelps, uncontrollably—for her. I finally said, "It's obvious you like Carmen. " His eyes glazed over and he blurted, "Like Her?" His friend interrupted and blurted back, "He's Obsessed With Her!!" It was hysterical watching his antics—he was a fun sideshow.

However, during the AI competition there was another personal favorite—there was this appealing kid from Raleigh, North Carolina with an amazing voice. When Carmen was voted off, my total adulation turned to Clay Holmes Aiken. This 24-year old caught me off guard. I not only voted for him I stood in front of my TV, cheering and clapping and throwing my applause at the screen—"Yes! Yes! Way to go. Brilliant!!" Then after the judging, my jeers and attacks were hurled at Simon. "You're a jerk!"

During each "Aiken for Clay" performance, I called my married children to see if they were watching. My daughter Heidi, said she had heard about the show, because one of her clients said she liked Ruben. I yelled, "Tell her to vote for Clay!" Marty, my daughter-in-law, when the phone rang after each show, she'd say to the children, "That's Grandma!" I would get my son Mike on the phone every Tuesday and Wednesday night, post performances and verify his/my thoughts On Clay verses Ruben. He soon just agreed with me that "to Clay or not to Clay" that was the question. He always "to Clay'd" me—just "to quiet his mother. However, my children and their spouses were becoming concerned.

Brett, Mark and Courtney made a connective call and inquired, "Mother! Are you all right?" They seriously questioned if I were going thru a Mid-Life-Crisis. But they knew I was a happy single and I had become suspect because most men my age were looking for a "Nurse and a Purse."

I assured them "this will soon pass." But it didn't. The 2003 *American Idol*-ride became a fun weekly adrenalin rush. The cheering continued, "Good for you Clay!" Then, "You showed 'em!" Then, "Sing your heart out guy!" then "Take that Simon!" My low blood pressure climbed and I acted outside of myself but that became the norm. However, the reality—millions of other women (and men) were acting just like me. So the world and I continued our fixation for Clay Aiken Holmes with adoration and without apology.

Gaye Deamer

5230

Blends Created By Bonnie Wallace

CHAPTER TEN

I think the people who did the best on the show were the
people who had the best sense of...this is about winning
and...about competing. Yes, I'm going to have fun. Yes, I'm
going to make some friends. It's going to be a neat experience
for me, but I am...here with a purpose—
to get the job done.

—Clay Aiken

CLAY'S JOURNEY TO STARDOM

Ryan. Seacrest reminded the viewers of Clay's *American Idol* gamble. "It was his Senior year at The University of North Carolina in Charlotte when Clay decided to drive to the *American Idol* auditions in Atlanta and roll the dice. Clay didn't look like a Pop Star, but he sure had the confidence of one." Aiken walked in and stood before Rome, who dismisses the condemned like sprayed flies in a sieve. He faked self-assurance but admitted he was very nervous because he had just been cut when he auditioned in Charlotte. The probable cause—Clay's curious appearance did not fit the image of a Pop Star. However, he acted like he belonged—not to the Roman Empire, but merely as Clayton Holmes Aiken. The Idol judges were doe-eyed and heavy-lidded from the thousands of jesters who had siphoned through their iron gates for a chance at stardom. They could hardly muster wordage as they looked at this unusual-looking contestant—No. 5230.... They were assuredly thinking, "Next."

Simon asked, "Why are you here?"

Clay gestured boldly, "I'm the *American Idol*!"

Clay didn't believe he was the *American Idol*, but Simon had previously told the large group of contestants if they didn't brim with confidence they would get cut. The 24-year-old College kid said later that he was surprised what came out of his mouth. However, Clay's friends said they weren't a bit surprised because he always displayed that kind of self-assurance. But Aiken confessed, he didn't think he had a chance because he had witnessed a number of first-rate singers get eliminated.

Simon asked Clay if he had watched the first *American Idol*. Aiken said, "Yes."

He had only seen a few shows but he had seen enough to witness Simon's cruel assaults. When Simon asked him what his thoughts were concerning last year's show, Clay said he thought he could have gotten to number one or two, at least.

The judges stared.

Clay sang.... "And we'll share tomorrow together."

Simon said he did not look like a Pop Star but he had a great voice.

Randy. "Yah, weird, it's wild."

Randy and Simon both agreed the kid could sing.

Simon. "Clayton, see you in Hollywood. Congratulations!"

Aiken's Hollywood hair went from red to black to mahogany to brown to spiked as he battled to stay in each round. He made it into the top 32 and turned a cartwheel for the world to see. Regardless, the cartwheel fell flat because when the votes were tallied for Group 2, he was eliminated. America gave the highest votes to Ruben Studdard and Kimberly Locke. Clay was wounded, but the bandages came off quickly when he was voted back into the Top 12 as a Wild Card.... Simon said Clay's Wild Card performance was the best, up to that point of the competition. Randy Jackson gave a standup applause with, "Brilliant Dawg, just brilliant!" And Paula Abdul said Clay surprised her every time he opened his mouth because he had such an amazing tone.... At this interlude the populace couldn't ignore this Clay-Original, who had no professional voice training. (Imagine what most of us would surrender for that kind of bestowal.)

Then a wave of support started to swell as Clay's growing electorate began adopting him as their personal prodigy. Clay indicated on Larry King Live that all of those who were voted in the top 12 were very talented people. Clay has always been charitable in his praise of his competitors, but the AI competition could not even begin to compete with the Web entries logging onto Cyberspace for this North Carolina singer.

Keep in mind before *American Idol*; Clay Aiken could hardly muster a date. Presently, every girl who has turned him down now stutters over her rejection. With good reason.

Clay Aiken has become a phenomenon. His every mouth gesture is worshipped. Every look on his slightly freckled face and every whisper to the judges of "thank you very much" has been immortalized. And "Look at that adorable smile, especially when it curves to one side." And "I want his baby." (What baby?). "And did you notice that luminous crown that shone on his head when he sang that brilliant rendition of 'Solitaire' that left Neil Sedaka and the rest of the world, in tears." I cried too and I am a grownup.

Clayton Holmes Aiken had no idea what was taking place outside the *American Idol* Mansion. He had no clue that every song he had ever sung was being pirated off the Internet and home office CD burners were billowing with CD pirated smoke. His songs were being played and replayed so many times, it suggested many power bills went on overload. The Clay fantasies took control of the air spaces from Canada to Hong Kong.

Some compared it to Beatle Mania; others said there would never be another Beatle Mania. However, that subject is up for grabs. Even so, at the peak of their popularity the Beatles made a stupefied snafu when they announced on the International Airways they were more popular than Jesus. Their halos thundered to the ground as their fans were in disbelief. Their popularity was never the same, but The Beatles had their Universal Season that many believe can never be duplicated, plus each Beatle has gone his separate way. Tragically, two of the Beatle's lives were shortened. A gunman stole John Lennon's life—and George Harrison's life was lost to the big C— (cancer). I'll bet John and George are still singing—Paul McCartney certainly is (he's also a new father) and the world still offers its admiration, especially because their will never be another Paul McCartney.

Blends Created By Bonnie Wallace

CHAPTER ELEVEN

The fact Simon's critical assessments dominate the judge's corner, it also supports Simon's own personal genre of self-carved creation. However, with his self-carved nemesis that targets other people, he also needs to circle his wagons.

Victory belongs to the most persevering

Napoleon

THE REMARKABLE TRANSFORMATION OF CLAY HOLMES AIKEN

Clay's persona is magical (via Gladys Knight)—he rarely looks the same. He is the "the singer with a thousand faces." However, it's not just his face—the parcel of Clay resembles an evolutionistic constellation of Argo Navis. His face and appearance change so dramatically if you saw the individual persons of Clay Holmes Aiken walking down the street, you would swear they were not even related.

To begin—Clay's *American Idol* audition was double take and mouth gape. When this librarian look-alike introduced himself as the next *American Idol* with his pallid face, jug ears, greased mahogany hair, rimmed magnifying glasses and his perennial striped shirt hanging over baggy tan pants, the viewer expressions cloned the deadpan look of the judges. Everyone became quiet, and I also cloned the mutterings, "The next *American Idol*? Dream on Kid!" I crunched my upper lip and wished Joshua Gracin would walk on stage and give another military salute—now that turned me on.

Then the next shot zeros in on this Aiken kid crawling on his knees, jumping up and down—imitating gyrating jumping jacks, giggling hysterically and turning cartwheels with the other hopefuls because he and his giddy friends were chosen to go to Hollywood—the yelping cartwheel frame was actually when he made it in the AI top 32. After that, the subsequent frame shows this 16 year-old Elvis look-alike with black hair and carved black side burns and it appears that Aiken has shrunk 6 inches—this former 6 foot 1 inch tall gangly replicated teen qualifies that Elvis is alive. Next, Clay Jr.—this 14 year old, 5 foot 5 inch, fan-eared boy sits, holding hands with the other contestants in a periwinkle shirt with gelled dark brown hair that proves he has discovered the fountain of youth. This confirms with each segment Aiken's getting younger in height and age.

Regardless, at this point in the competition Clay had advanced the top three of Group 2, then lost to Ruben Studdard and Kimberly Locke. Aiken was out of the competition. However, the nine contestants who had been cut were given another chance to try and win a Wild Card spot to make it in *American Idol*'s top 12. Four slots were up for grabs. The three judges would each choose one Wild Card favorite and the American voters would add the last contestant. So the guy from Raleigh, North Carolina had another chance to get back in the game.

So, "Here comes Aiken" again—where? Where's that Chameleon? That can't be Aiken—this 24 year old, 6 foot 1 inch sharp guy in a trendy black sports suit and iridescent white teeth—where did those teeth come from? Regardless, Clay walks on stage with the confidence of a ringmaster and sings "Don't Let The Sun Go Down On Me," for his Wild Card song. The judges' grin and the rest of us choke on our popcorn and we almost fall off our chairs. Who did you say that was? "That's Clay Aiken."

"That's who?" Where did that handsome guy come from? When he finished serenading me and the lines were open, I dropped my buttered popcorn and ran to the phone and voted. Don't think this is the end of the popcorn choking episodes, because the evolution has just begun. Aiken's transformation also includes the brutality he endured from the cruel judge, Simon Cowell. As a result, his fans picked up their shovels and helped tunnel a moat around the AI mansion for his protection.

Regardless, when Aiken finished his performance, the Judges raved. Randy and Paula gave him standing ovations. Paula said Clay had raised the bar. They said this is what the Wild Card is all about. Simon indicated his performance was up to that point, the best of the series.

In spite of the judges' fervor for Clay Aiken, Randy Jackson chose Kimberly Caldwell, 22 of Katy, Texas as his Wild Card pick. Caldwell, no stranger to contests, was a winner of "Star Search." and she was a finalist on WB's "Pop Stars." Plus, she has performed on stage (including Branson), most of her life.

Then, "Where's the extended applause for Clay Aiken?" Because Paula Abdul favored Trenyce—her given name, Lashundra Cobbins, another 22 year old who comes from Memphis, Tenn. Her powerful voice could not be dismissed— Trenyce deserved another chance.

Clay's hopes were dashed when Simon gave the judges last bid to Carmen Rasmussen, a 17 year old high school girl from Bountiful, Utah—a nod he gave enthusiastically. He thought she had a unique voice and indicated as mentioned, that Carmen was the most marketable of the female contestants. He favored Rasmussen from the beginning.

However, the three contestants chosen were calculated moves, because the judges knew whom the voters had selected as their Wild Card—Clay Holmes Aiken. The public had voted him back. *American Idol* therefore, had the four added competitors who could undeniably add some needed excitement and challenge to the contest.

Clay was no longer the kid with the fan ears—as the versatility of his performances emerged, his ears went under cover, as well as the horned rimmed glasses that were replaced with contact lenses. The makeover was so dramatic, the court no longer gawked at the redheaded, freckled face kid; they were in awe of Aiken's talent and his new dapper appearance. Everyone was so taken with his powerful rendition of "Don't Let The Sun Go Down On Me," they would not let the sun go down on Aiken because he had become a definite AI contender.

When Clay was ushered back in the competition, his mother Faye Parker said, "He's so cute, he's not only attractive to teenage girls, he's also appealing to middle age and to older ladies." (She was right.) She also said she thought Clayton could make it into *American Idol*'s top two. (She was right again.) Clay's mother was also impressed with his new look but she said, "I hoped it doesn't change him too much".... His fans laughed, "Mrs. Parker your son is a monarch of change."

Clay's evolving image mirrors the diversity of a bullfrog that has three kinds of highly branched colored cells that form separate discrete layers. The top layer displays xanthophores—yielding orange, red or yellow pigments; the middle layer is a silvery layer of pigment that reflects light; the bottom layer of skin has melanophonres showing black or brown melanin.... The rainbow of Clay Aiken continues to add its colors as we observe his metamorphosis. However, the second layer is already shining through as we uncover the journey of this American prodigy. A journey worth watching because no doubt,

we haven't seen the finish of Clay Aiken's "Amazing Race."
And shine he does.........

CA's First (top twelve) *American Idol* performance—This buffed-faced adorkable kid gave a winning energetic performance and two of the judges loved it—they both gave standing ovations—except you know who.

Let's continue with Clay's intuitive performances, but let's also chronicle the pattern of Simon Cowell's hyperbole critiques of Clay Aiken.

(The weekly critiques of Randy and Paula and most guest judges are not often included because they usually gave positive appraisal of Clay's performances; however, their occasional observations will be mentioned.)

Simon said, "If you've got a big mouth and you're controversial, you're going to get attention."

(1)—Tuesday: March 11: MOTOWN

(1)—Clay sang: "I Can't Help Myself." (The Simon slams begin.)
The duet and guest judge all gave him standing ovations.
Simon—Stone-faced said it sounded like a musical number from Motown. (NEGATIVE)

Clay was visibly crushed. He had watched "the crusher" on some segments of *American Idol* 2002, but the attacks had just begun....

(2)—Tuesday: March 18: SONGS FROM A MOVIE

(2)—Clay sang: "Somewhere Out There."
Randy and Paula and the stunning celebrity judge Gladys Knight loved it.
Simon indicated Clay was the one to beat. (POSITIVE)

Simon was right. Clay Aiken was the one to beat—his new-bronzed face and hair had females swooning. Clay admitted he didn't trust the AI fashion gurus in the beginning, but finally gave in to their suggestions as the allotted weekly clothing allowance adorned the singer with various shades of leather and pizzazz. As Aiken's talents were showcased, his fan base began to swell. A Raleigh radio station started sponsoring weekly screenings of *"American Idol"* at a local movie theatre, and the crowds lined up with their support. He not only had North Carolina shoring-up, sustenance of every age and description was building up in the dam. The lifeboats were organizing their strategies, plus there was dancing on the sand. Teeny boppers were stomping. Middle-age fans were bopping and Seniors were hopping for Clay Holmes Aiken—and the judges knew it.

Therefore, early in the competition, winning predictions were being announced by two of the judges. "You might as well end the competition now," Simon said in *Entertainment Weekly.* "You have to put your money on Clay. I just can't see anyone beating him at this point." When interviewed, Randy Jackson also confirmed, "For the record, I think Clay may win the whole thing."

While Simon was announcing on national television and in newspapers that Clay was the sure winner he continued pounding Aiken, week-after-week with "assault and battery." Randy and Paula were supportive and allowed some leeway in performance, but not Cowell. Heaven forbid if you misstep—watch out!

(3)—Tuesday: March 25—DISCO THEME SWITCHED TO COUNTRY ROCK

(3)—Clay sang: "Someone Else's Star."
Simon said that the performance was identical to last week and that Clay had just swapped songs. (NEGATIVE)

Simon Cowell did CA a favor—the critique was warranted. The theme was "Country Rock." Clay's performance was sung as a beautiful ballad. Regardless of the balladry, Clay realized he had to learn the ropes, because the embarrassing comments coming from SC could influence the audience and the winning outcome.

(4)—Tuesday: April 1: DISCO

After the previous week's dousing, the conservative Aiken came on stage with a shimmering brown polka dotted shirt and tan pants and really stepped-up with a great high energy performance. The kinder judges' and audience loved it.

(4)—Clay sang: "Everlasting Love."
Simon grimaced that he thought the performance was terrible." (NEGATIVE)

The criticism was ridiculous.... Clay masked his fears but he had reason to be afraid. There appeared to be a growing Cowellous resentment toward Clay—everyone and especially Aiken felt it. Was this resentment or strategy? Clay exuded so much confidence Paula praised him constantly for his self-assurance, but it was speculated that Cowell wanted to keep CA in his place. Also, (At this point forward, after each of Clay's performances— Simon turned around in his judges' chair and observed the rabid support growing for Aiken.) he adulation and posters for Clay filled the hall. One singer could not dominate the competition or the results would be too apparent and the enthusiasm for the show could diminish.

Simon said if the contestants think he is tough, the entertainment world is brutal.... Most contestants are greenies and Music Critics are infamous for prostrating mediocrity. Therefore, it is cognoscente to not let performers get too cocky. The job of the jury is to condition the kids for stardom and to keep the AI excitement and its guessing game on tract. Simon is not only the King Pin of cruelty; he is also a King Pin of viewer-ship. However, many questioned, "Why damage when constructive criticism could be more productive?" One celebrity judge indicated some of the contestants would probably need psychological counseling after being on the show.

Aiken did not dare expose injury. He admitted his self-assurance was on display to survive and confessed he was very frightened before every performance, but he didn't dare exhibit fear in front of the judges because he could get voted off. (Did you catch Clay's huge sighs of relief after every performance?) His fans all exhaled with him.

(5)—Tuesday: April 8: BILLBOARD #1 HITS

(5)—Clay sang: "At This Moment."

Randy and Paula didn't like the choice of song or the performance.

Guest Lionel Ritchie said he was in awe of what came out of "that body," and he felt Clay sang the song with great power and conviction and that he did a great job. However, collective negative reviews from all three *American Idol* judges, Randy, Paula and Simon could have been a problem for Aiken—look what happened to Tamyra Gray. Clay was a significant part of the contestant rivalry so Simon went against the duos negative reviews and added, "Keep Clay in the competition," appraisal.

Simon smiled that CA's performance was perfect and on the money! (POSITIVE)

(6)—Tuesday: April 15— BILLY JOEL SONGS

Clay introduced his next song standing on the inside-steps of the AI mansion with a tangerine complexion, tangerine cow-licked hair, tangerine eyebrows and an orange shirt. This portrait of Clay wouldn't have been easily recognized outside the Idol mansion. He didn't even resemble the guy who later walked on stage in a razor-sharp black suit with a blue "T," with perfectly spiked brown hair and perfectly spiked matching eyebrows. His fans admit, "The latter is the one of the many Clay Aiken faces they are gah, gah, over."

(6)—Clay sang: "Tell Her About It."
Simon sneered— he preferred Aiken's performances when he closed his eyes! He indicated Clay's exaggerated facial expressions were distracting. (NEGATIVE—unnecessarily cruel.)

Aiken's increasing exaggerated facial lexis needed calming, admittedly. The critique could have been offered more kindly, but stay on your toes kid because by the time Slimon gets through with you, you will know the meaning of intentional humiliation. Simon swore what he said was a compliment. The audience was furious.

(7)—Tuesday: April 22— DIANE WARREN SONGS

The award winning Diane Warren has many plaudits to her credit with an impressive music portfolio. Clay chose, "I Could Not Ask For More," originally sung by Edwin McCain and Sarah Evans. However, Aiken not only had to make each song his own, he had to correct the side mouth curves, the exaggerated facial expressions and the multiple Simon jabs from the week before and the week before and the week before and....
Elites TV wrote, "Clay made a concerted effort to stop the 'weird faces and eye flutters' that Cowell mentioned in the previous week's competition, changed his wardrobe to reflect the gradual change that he has made from 'Geek to Chic.' He continues to master dramatic stage presence, and knows he owns the stage, without coming off as arrogant."

(7)—Clay sang: "I Could Not Ask For More."
Randy said he felt Clay was one of the best in America.

Paula indicated he was a serious contender.

Diane Warren raved and said she loved his voice— "wonderful, beautiful, excellent."

Simon stuttered and then downplayed the three previous judges' adulation by telling Clay he was not the type of recording artist they were looking for and he would do better on Broadway. (NEGATIVE—unnecessarily cruel.)

The audience went ballistic and booed Simon's stutters. Diane Warren gave Cowell a black "T" shirt that read, "Sorry, but I don't do nice." Simon seldom does nice and he thrives on his solanaceous attacks. But most people are nice. While Aiken was trying to beat the odds, his family was offering unconditional support. Clay's younger Brother Brett Parker, then 17, said he supports whatever choice his big brother makes. "As long as he gets to do what he wants, I'm happy." Brett and his friends decorated their cars with "Vote for Clay" signs and drew supportive honks from motorists near their Raleigh high school. His mother and older brother and sister, Jeff and Amy were appalled, as they witnessed the lashings.

(8-9) Tuesday: April 29—NEAL SEDAKA'S 60's—TUNES

Neal Sedaka one of the great singers and songwriters of the 60's sold over 40 million records by the age of 24--a record unprecedented by any standard. Some of his songs are considered real classics. "Solitaire," is hailed as one of the most beautiful songs ever written. Neal Sedaka recognized Clay's incredible talent from the get-go and gave him enthusiastic reviews.

(8)—Clay sang: "Buttercup."

Randy said he did a great job and he was entertained.

Neal Sedaka told Clay he sings like Andre Agasi plays tennis. He said his performance was perfection and then added that he would kill to write and produce Aiken's first CD.

Paula complimented him on his spirit dancing.

Simon skirted his critique because CA gave a great high-energy performance and it was rumored that he knew Clay's next performance "Solitaire" was magnum opus. ("Don't shower too much praise SC, because remember Clay Aiken is not what you are looking for.") He asked Aiken with a scowell on his face, "What does Buttercup mean?
(NO CRITIQUE)

(9)—Clay sang, "Solitaire."
Randy was very impressed.
Neal Sedaka with tears in his eyes gave "Bravos to Clay," and said he had lost his song forever because, "Solitaire" would always be a Clay Aiken song.
Paula loved it and said Clay was now a Pop Singer. (She was offsetting the continuous "Clay was Broadway" innuendos from Simon Cowell.)
Simon said CA was one of the few people in the competition who could take criticism like a grownup and said he applied the criticism to improve his performances. He emphasized, "That was a fantastic performance." (POSITIVE)

(10-11)—Tuesday: May 6— BEE GEES TUNES
This night they sang two songs: (10 and 11.)

(10)—Clay Sang: "To Love Somebody."
Simon: "Probably one of the best performances I've ever heard throughout the entire competition. (POSITIVE)
Fans said Simon raved about "To Love Somebody" because he knew he could take it all back with Clay's next performance of "Grease." This accusation flooded the Internet. Their reasoning—See Vincent below, that qualifies the judges know ahead of time regarding the quality of each performance.

(11)—Clay sang: "Grease."
Simon paused dramatically and said everything about "Grease," was "Horrible," and he kept repeating "Horrible." SC

said Clay blew away his first performance—because he didn't like his second performance.... How does "having a little fun with one performance" ERASE a previous brilliant performance? Doesn't each performance stand on its own merit? WHAT MAGICAL ERASER DOES Simon Cowell POSSES? (NEGATIVE)

Tuesday: May 13—RANDOM/JUDGES/CONTES-TANTS FAVORITES
This night they sang three songs: (12, 13 and 14).

(12)—Clay sang: "Vincent"
Randy and Paula said it wasn't his best and Paula indicated he forgot the words.
Simon said it was a dreary rendition and that it was terrible." (NEGATIVE)

This performance had the airwaves on fire. The story: Vincent was changed 25 minutes before Clay was to sing it live. The judges had not heard the change when they watched the pre-show rehearsal. When Clay paused during his performance, the judges thought he had forgotten the words. Clay took their criticism without comment but he was very upset back stage. The Producers explained to the audience that the song had been changed, possibly to pacify Clay. A further explanation—the producers added a verse to "Vincent" because the show was running too short. Too short? The lag time in the song was exactly 12 seconds. Ryan Seacrest could have "burped" and made up the difference.

Another Vincent version.... Michael Orland the AI pianist/musician said he would take blame for the blunder. He said each of the three songs the contestants were to sing that night were 4 1/2 minutes long. Clay did not like Vincent so he, Clay and Debra Byrd decided to make Vincent shorter. But the execs were not happy with the change; so just before the live show they had to add another verse. Regardless, everyone was told what had happened. Why was Clay targeted and the blame rocketed immediately to every News and Entertainment show in the country that "the nerves were getting to Clay," because during one of his performances poor Clay had forgotten the words to his song?

(13)—Clay sang: "Mack The Knife."
Randy and Paula gave CA a standing ovation.
Simon said the rendition was brilliant and amazing. (POS-ITIVE)

(14)—Clay sang: "Unchained Melody."
Paula said forthright that "Unchained Melody" was best performance of the entire competition.
Simon countered Paula's rave review. He said he didn't agree with her appraisal because he thought Clay's performance was "over the top." (NEGATIVE—then as Clay stood there—a forced very good, well done.

Just before the finals Simon Cowell was on Regis and Kelly promoting his new show "*Cupid.*" He was asked whom he thought was going to win *American Idol* and Cowell said, "Ruben Studdard." Surprise, surprise, surprise. That had to be a real shocker.

Tuesday: May 20: ONE ORIGINAL and TWO COVERS (Songs previously recorded by another artist.)
The night of the finals they sang three songs: (15, 16, and 17).

(15)—Clay sang: "This Is The Night."
Simon: Finals Night Reviews in To "Fix Or Not To Fix" chapter. (NEGATIVE)

(16)—Clay sang: "Here There And Everywhere."
Simon: Finals Night Reviews in "To Fix Or Not To Fix"

chapter. (NEUTRAL)

(17)—Clay sang: "Bridge Over Troubled Water."
Simon: Finals Night reviews in "To Fix Or Not To Fix" chapter. (POSITIVE)

A RECAP OF THE AMERICAN IDOL JOURNEY

October 2002
-26— Clay auditioned in Atlanta, singing the Luther Vandross hit "Always and Forever." He became one of 234 contestants chosen to go to Hollywood.
January 2003
-21—The "*American Idol*" broadcast begins.
-29—Clay made it to the top 32 contestants.
February
-11—Aiken sang "Open Arms" by Journey—one of eight performers.
-12—Ruben Studdard and Kimberly Locke were chosen to advance to the finals from Clay's Group 2. Clay was eliminated.
March
-4—Aiken sang Elton John's "Don't Let the Sun Go Down on Me," competing for the Wild Card.
Clay was chosen as the voter's Wild Card choice.
-11— Clay sang the Four Tops hit "I Can't Help Myself" for Motown night.
-12—Vanessa Olivarez was voted off.
-18—Aiken performed "Somewhere Out There" from "An American Tale," a song chosen from the Movie theme.
-19— Charles Grigsby was eliminated.
-25—Clay sang "Some One Else's Star," for his Country Rock pick.
-26— Julia DeMato was sent home.
-28— Simon told *Entertainment Weekly* magazine, "You have

to put your money on Clay. I just can't see anyone beating him at this point."

April

-1— Clay sang, "Everlasting Love" for his disco number.

-2—Corey Clark was sent home after the producers learn about (non-disclosed) assault charges filed against him. Charges were later dropped.

-8—Clay performed "At This Moment" by Billy Vera, for his "No.1 Hits" rendition.

-9—Rickey Smith was eliminated.

-15—Clay sang Billy Joel's, "Tell Her About It".

-16—Kimberly Caldwell was sent home to Katy.

-22— Clay performed Diane Warren's "I Could Not Ask For More."

-23— Carmen Rasmussen was voted off.

-29—Four contestants were left to compete for the title, each one performed two numbers. Clay sang and danced to "Build Me Up Buttercup" (a 60's UK song), later he performed, "Solitaire" (Neil Sedaka's own).

-30— Trenyce was eliminated.

May

-6— Clay shone with "To Love Somebody," soon after he gyrated his hips to "Grease."

-7— Joshua Gracin marched back to the Marine base, leaving Clay Aiken of Raleigh, North Carolina, Ruben Studdard of Birmingham, Alabama and Kimberley Locke of Nashville, Tennessee. The two contenders, who made the cut on Feb. 12, were again his competition for the top final three.

-8— Clay went home to Raleigh for a whirlwind tour of the Triangle. He landed in a helicopter in the middle of the playing field, performed the "National Anthem," and threw out the first pitch before a Durham Bulls game. He also had a meeting with Gov. Mike Easley.

-13—Clay sang Don McLean's "Vincent. " He also belted "Mack the Knife," and gave a final breathtaking performance of "Unchained Melody."

-14— Clay and Ruben are voted as the two top *American Idol* finalists.

Kimberly Locke was eliminated.

-20—The Finals: Clay sang, "This is the Night," also the Beatles' "Here, There and Everywhere;" and for his third song Simon and Garfunkel's "Bridge Over Troubled Water," that brought the house down. Judge Simon says his closing song may win him the competition.

-21—He was not declared the winner, by a margin of a 134,400 votes. The claim was a discrepancy of 50.28% for Ruben and 49.72% for Clay— out of 24 million votes cast; Ruben becomes the new *"American Idol."*

THE GROUP SONGS PERFORMED:

1. Heat Wave
2. Footloose
3. Where The Black Top Ends
4. Boogie Wonderland
5. All Night Long
6. God Bless The USA (Studio Version)
7. Time Of My Life
8. God Bless the USA
9. Shine
10. One Voice
11. Judge's Medley Of Songs
12. Final Three

Whatsoever thy hand findeth to do,
Do it with thy might.

ECCLESIASTES. IX. 10

CHAPTER TWELVE

You can fool some of the people all of the time,
and all of the people some of the time,
but you cannot fool all of the people
all of the time.

Lincoln

TO FIX OR NOT TO FIX—
THAT IS THE QUESTION??

The AI2 roller coaster was a whirlwind for most voters. It could have been a satisfying end to the popular TV show but the last week of the contest turned into a finality of disbelief. Because people do not like being jerked around.

Clay's militia had organized a sure-fire strategy for him to win. There were multitudes of websites where thousands of fans pledged to vote non-stop during the two-to-three hour vigils. Most phones, with the push of a button "redials automatically" when pushed again, it "redials." After hours of pressing the button non-stop, the voters admitted their fingers became numb, but the reward was immediate because the friendly voice kept repeating, "Thanks for voting for Contestant No.1 or 2 or..." That friendly voice talked to the willing volunteers all night. Most people will work their hearts out for a mere "Thank You," and the Claymates were no exception. Finally, after much pain-staking effort, the two finalists were chosen—Clay Aiken and Ruben Studdard. But, the audience was also smitten with Kimberly Locke—a gorgeous girl with a stunning voice. Her voice resonates like a fine-tuned instrument when she hits the higher range of song that leaves you in awe—an amazing talent. However, Ruben had lucked-out because he had previously been in the bottom two for tallying the fewest number of votes. As a result, Aiken's tract record indicated he was the next *American Idol*— the evidence was everywhere. Clay was never in the bottom two. The World-Wide-Web proved he was the winner if you compare his hits on the web were four times higher than his competition. Plus, Clay's CD climbed to No.1 the first 12 hours of advertised pre-release compared to his competitor who logged in at No. 386. Clay's CD dominated the No.1 spot from day one. The undisputed loyalty of the Claymates, Clayboard, Clack, Clayniacs, Claynations, Claynadians, Claytrain, and the Clay-you-name-its, gave the crown to the deictic *American Idol*.... The number's game is king in the World of Music. But don't count on it! The ploy of Aiken's defoliation was in full bloom.

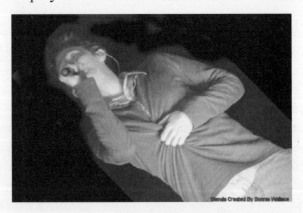

A week before the finals the Entertainment News Programs were inundated with Ruben Studdard. There was almost no mention of Clay Aiken. The fans were in disbelief, "What is going on? Why don't they mention Clay?" This was not a one-man race. Maybe if they ignore this great kid, no one will vote for him. But that is already taken care of. "Right?" The cyber boards shouted, "You know if there is supposed to be a contest, "Let's have a contest. If the game is sloped, it shouldn't be done so advertently—people are watching."

Regardless, other media voiced their Clay predictions in spite of what the TV Entertainment Channels were flaunting. Before the finals a *MSNBC* staff writer reported, "If Monday's night's show (an AI Special) is any indication, Aiken may already be in the winner's circle. The Raleigh native served up a smokin' rendition of 'Don't Let the Sun Go Down on Me,' a song that helped get him back in the 'Idol' competition."

The Washington-based business intelligence and marketing firm *New Media Strategy* put out a news release forecasting a close Aiken win.... Those observing the Aiken camps never thought it was going to be a neck n' neck race because of the evidence and because of the collective winning strategies of Clay's army.

Also, Simon then told *Newsweek* that Aiken "will win by a whisker." Then Cowell with the other side of his mouth discredited Clay to other media. But, how can you show genuine favoritism to someone who was groomed all along to be the 2nd place Runner up?

The Night Of The Finals....
The Clowns came out—the Circus began.

Clay's performance of "This Is The Night," was superb. Randy Jackson and Paul Abdul raved. Randy said even though he didn't particularly like the song, Clay sang his face off. . Paula agreed with Randy and said that he nailed every song every week.

Then the Judge in the perennial black T-Shirt opens his perennial black mouth. Simon grinned and told Clay how handsome the show had made him. Clay was charged with beamish laughter. A compliment on the finals night from Simon? Wow! Then Cowell smirked and indicated that he wasn't being rude but said how **ugly** Clay was when he auditioned for *American Idol*—the audience and other judges were shocked! The antagonist then indicated that what he had said was a compliment because the show had made him handsome. Clay took the constant degradation always like a gentleman from this black t-shirt nightmare. Most people have questioned—where does this guy come from? Simon confessed on *Oprah* that he felt abandoned as a child because he was sent to a boarding school at a very young age and he added that growing up his mother never hugged or kissed him. His brother said he was a Wannabe Star. He said Simon used to stand in front of a mirror using a hairbrush as a pretend microphone and would try to sing, but he said it was pathetic watching him.

Regardless, the tyrant continued to demean Clay Aiken, after the " comment...he said he didn't like the song because it sounded liked an *American Idol* Musical. He said he thought Clay was capable of better. Capable of better? Better at what? Better at being ugly? Better at nailing the song every week? Better at "Singing Your Face off?" What? Simon's obvious ploy (his Aiken ploys are glaringly transparent at this stage of the game) was to reinforce in the minds of the American voters repeatedly, that Clay was still Mr. Broadway. The audience loved the performance. Black t-shirt mendacity--the crowd agreed.

Simon admitted in an interview with *Newsweek*. "What you are trying to do, if you can, is tell the audience who you want to be in the finals. You're not getting accurate judging. You're not." Then he later said, "My attitude has always been, don't lie to people!" The contestants and voters were obviously confused.

In spite of the judge, the audience loved Clay's rendition of

"This Is The Night," so much, thousands of fans e-mailed RCA and requested the song as his first CD. RCA complied (The "breaking news," the TITN CD the one Simon said, "I think you're capable of better," went platinum (one million CD's shipped) in 37 days, breaking all previous records in history, except for the Elton John/Princess Diana tribute.)

The night of the finals Clay and Ruben were exhausted from the four months of non-stop performances and demands. They hid their fatigue, because this night would determine who would win the *American Idol* Crown. Clay tried to bring a mixed variety to his three-song requirement.... His second performance of "Here, There And Everywhere," a Paul McCartney ballad was dreary and speculation was, his face was made to look ghastly to further discredit his performance. While he sang, a sickening shadow was layered on Clay Aiken's face. The hideous wingspan made Clay look like he had a facial disease. Lighting experts know what they are doing.... This author wrote and produced a Touring Musical. In staging the show, technicians were hired to produce the lighting wizardry we desired. When the actors required Phantom Faces, these experts created Phantom faces—they designed kaleidoscopic magic for perfect results. Clay Aiken was not only humiliated every week in front of millions of people; his face was made to look grotesque while he sang his second song—alleged manipulation appeared on the big screen.

The Saboteurs were accused of trying everything to demote Aiken because The Kid was rumored to bring the house down with his 3rd and final performance" AND THE KID DID. Clay gave a show-stopping rendition of, "A Bridge Over Troubled Waters," that had Randy and Paula and the rest of the world on their feet. Paula verified, "Clay, this is your personal best!" and of course Simon said, "I thought you were off tonight," but then admitted, "That performance could win you the competition!"

Everyone knew Clay had clinched it, even nervous Ruben fans thought that performance would give the Crown to Clay Aiken. Clay had done everything he could to win—now his voting fans would "bring it!" This is what his fans had worked for, day and night, month after month to help him secure—his title of *American Idol*.

His gargantuan fan base, would vote for Clay Holmes Aiken until their fingers fell off and mine almost did. This self-determination was out of my own realm of ever wanting to do anything so superfluous. It awakened a sense of, "What are you spending your time doing this for? I didn't know and I didn't care. I was a willing volunteer."

The consensus—Clay was a southern gentleman with a stunning voice. This North Carolina kid was amazed that people even liked him. He had a tough time getting a date; he helped special needs kids; he always honored his mother; he sang mostly in high school choirs and local productions. Clay Aiken was an exceptional young man who deserved this chance at Stardom. Clay sang his heart out week after week to beat the odds; the UK bully degraded him relentlessly and it touched me so deeply; I bequeathed my time and joined the battle for his victory.

However, the voting for the finals was three solid hours. Heaven Help Us! How would our fingers survive the three-hour grind? The show ended. The dialing began. The instructions were to place a pad and pen next to the telephone to record the votes.... The first fifteen minutes of dialing and redialing— not one vote.... The first half hour of dialing and redialing— where was that friendly voice? ONE SOLID HOUR OF DIALING AND REDIALING—NOT ONE SINGLE SOLITARY VOTE. Hour after hour the voters dialed and redialed— most attempts for Clay-nothing. I personally pushed redial for 2 1/2 hours before getting one measly vote. Most voters tried for 3 solid hours and their reward—the busy signal.... BUT WAIT! This was great news. This had to be a Clay Aiken voting frenzy. He had definitely won, because many had tried Ruben's line and his votes went through.... Everyone was ecstatic!

The night of the finals the voters were anxious for the CA

crowning. Then Ryan Seacrest announced, "The 2003 new *American Idol* is...Ruben Studdard!" The euphoria turned to disbelief. How could this be? THE INTERNATIONAL RAGE BEGAN! In comparing notes, most of Clay's lines were jammed, while most of Ruben fans were able to vote all night long. A thunderous rage was heard around the globe, including Canada, England, Singapore and numerous other countries— that could not even vote.

Two frustrated fans said they started keeping track. They got (1) vote for Clay about every 165 attempts, and got (1) vote for Ruben every 12 dials.... A spokesperson for SBC, a major service provider, says, "Who gets through is a completely Random Process." Random scam-dom. The critics questioned the process and so did the millions of Clay Aiken fans.

During the three-hour voting marathon, the instant dialing/redialing was clocked. It was reported a person could redial twice every five seconds. The second the busy signal was heard the redial button was hit. So every 60 seconds = 24 redials. Therefore, 3 hours =180 minutes X 24 redials= 4320 ATTEMPTS COULD BE MADE TO VOTE IN A 3 HOUR PERIOD, if the voice of "thank you" wasn't heard. Many voters dialed up to 4,000 times and could not register (1) derisory vote. "Hell hath no fury like females and yes! males who hath put forth that kind of effort and discover they have been taken for a 3-hour, horsey ride...."

The voters asked Mr. SBC to please define random. Webster's Dictionary says "random" is, "Lack of definite direction or aim or intention without definite purpose or aim; hap-hazardly." They challenged, "Based on Webster's definition, how could anyone have been declared a winner?"

The owner of a telemarketing company bragged, on the night of the finals he set 200 phones on auto-dial and registered over 250,000 hits for Studdard. Ruben's mother said she voted over 200 times for her son and his grandmother got through 7 times. Then an 11-year-old Ruben fan announced he completed 700 calls. However, Clay's mother tried non-stop and was never put through—not once. Plus, some fans were furious, because when they tried to vote for Clay, their calls went to Ruben.

An Indiana Company reported their telephone number was only one-digit away from *American Idol*'s toll-free number and they were inundated with calls. Their system received 241,496 calls from all over the country from fans who thought they were voting for their favorite contestant. They said Clay Aiken received twice as many votes as his competitor. The misdialed calls gave Clay Aiken 169,382 votes and Ruben 72,114 votes. The Contest Execs announced immediately that when they added the misdialed tallies, "Ruben still won." The winning difference out of 24 million calls was only 134,400 votes (50.28% verses 49.72%). When Clay's votes were allowed to get through they were double that of his competition, plus millions of Clay's votes were never registered. What is wrong with this picture? A Chemistry buff was asked to take this baffler to a Chem Lab to put it under the microscope. No wait! "Rigged" isn't Chemistry. Then what? A mathematician was then approached—maybe the solution is in Rigonometry. Nope.... Since Clay's lines were dead, it was obviously Rigormortis....

The critic's corner implied that Fox would never manipulate results because it would threaten their franchise, but they admitted the outcome appeared to be very suspicious. *American Idol* Co-Executive Producer Nygel Lythgoe, said controversy has never hurt the show.

Besides, Ruben Studdard has endeared himself to a bevy of devoted fans. They love his velvet voice and those high-cheeked dimples. The bond he and Aiken developed was refreshing.They often pretended to duke-it-out with fake stomach punches and jibes. The unlikely mismatch has made AI history because *American Idol* will undoubtedly never duplicate these two-at-the-top.

In spite of their friendship, Clay Aiken not only got the Royal Shaft (the Royal Shaft proved to be in Aiken's favor) but many have felt badly for the genuinely nice guy from

Birmingham because the results are still highly questioned. Clay Aiken, the gracious loser told Ruben and the audience in the final minutes of the show, "I'm going to beat him up later for stealing my title." Of course, the parroted consensus is, "He didn't steal your title, the title was stolen from you."

The media reported: Carol Costello, *CNN* Anchor: "It came as a shock to many. Ruben Studdard awoke this morning from what must have seemed a dream. As you just saw, he was crowned the new *'American Idol'* after a show stopping finale with 'Idol hopeful Clay Aiken.'"

Plus, Newspapers and Magazines across the country with front cover questions and concerns continued the probe:

Us Weekly Magazine's Cover Story, Challenged the results:
"I didn't lose," says Clay"
"Ruben vs Clay"
"DID THE RIGHT MAN WIN?"
"Who'll make more money?"
"Why the battle's not over"

In Touch Weekly Magazine's Cover Story, also disputed the outcome:

"WAS IT FIXED?"
"WHY FANS ARE DEMANDING A RECOUNT!"
"RUBEN: Did he really win?"
"CLAY: Was he robbed?"

Interestingly, *In Touch* Magazine is reported to be tied to the Fox conglomerate. As a result, they nobly addressed the public's outrage. Their marketing controversy keeps the fires burning.

Regardless, here are samples of some of the thousands of protests:

Kimberly Munro in Seattle wrote that she dialed non-stop for Clay Aiken for three hours and never registered a single vote. Out of curiosity she dialed Ruben's number and got through on the first try. Her mother in Las Vegas also dialed for the full three hours for Clay and made it through twice. Like her daughter she tried Ruben's number and was connected immediately. Munro asked, "If it was easy to get through to Ruben's line and nearly impossible to get through to Clay's for the full 3 hours, how did Ruben win?"

Martha Price Stokes used two phones dialing every few seconds for more than three hours, and she couldn't complete a single call.... Her husband in Fort Lauderdale, Fla. and daughter in Spring Hope also dialed in vain. Cleary continues.... "The crowning of Studdard as America's 'Idol' has produced in many local Aiken fans a level of confusion and outrage on the order of that 2000 election...and cries of a fix."

Below are additional samplings of non-stop complaints:

Two sisters tried all night and only got to vote 5 times.... "The results of the show could in no way represent popular opinion. I think Clay's #02 is encrypted into my redial from the amount of times I tried to call with no avail."

Re: Voting Fiasco. "I hit the re-dial button on my phone NON—STOP for 3 straight hours and did NOT get (1) vote for Clay...I feel cheated that I couldn't participate in the final outcome after having voted and watched all season!"

Another: "I am outraged! Clay Aiken truly got the shaft. I would embrace Ruben if this had been on the up and up.... I am furious at the amount of effort that was thrown at Clay Aiken and our efforts were totally dismissed."

Caitlin Cleary a Staff Writer (newsobserver.com) reports that: Patricia Hyatt, a real estate agent from Raleigh, called Tuesday night only to hear: "All circuits are busy at this time."

The outrage continued as—The circuit clowns kept their juggling act going for (3) solid hours.... Then the monkeys swung down from the high bars, the elephants gave their final curtsy, and the big cats bellowed their closing growl. And the winner is....

The SBC Spokesman said, "Callers had no problems once they got past local exchanges to the AT&T national line." The voters were furious, then questioned, "Were Ruben's lines colored Ebony and Clay's painted Ivory? Or were the phone lines all Ebonized with no exchanges left for the Ivory Tower? That would be a reasonable glitch to fix or was it merely bait and switch?

The public is not clueless—cyberspace has made them savvy and smart. With the click of a mouse, new-age information is at their fingertips. As a result, the Claymates can track the day-to-day (oft times, hour-to-hour) progress of their *American Idol*. And they do. And they knew....

Before the finals, Clay's CD had broken all presales records at Amazon—Aiken's CD was selling four times faster than his competition. Also Clay's web entries were four times higher. (They are now five times higher.) In 2003, Lycos 50 reported that Clay Aiken was the third most-highly searched male on the Internet.

Regardless, the powers in charge were pulling for Studdard and everybody knew it—he received non-stop accolades from all three judges with every performance. Simon admitted in his "Rude" book that he had been so sycophantic (flattering) toward Ruben that he personally had almost run out of compliments. This confused the audience because many comments from viewers were "most of Ruben's songs sounded the same." One Columnist wrote he liked Ruben but "his performances were same old, same old." In addition, what was odd— none of the judges ever criticized Ruben's weight; the way he dressed— how his 6 XL shirts hung to his knees or how he sweats. This comparison is only necessary to level the playing field because Simon's criticism of Aiken never stopped. He grimaced that Clay was too Broadway and not the type they were looking for and how he preferred Clay with his eyes closed. He indicated how CA had big feet and how he his suit made him look like a waiter, and how ugly he was when he auditioned for AI. (After the finals and Ruben won, Simon still hurled the ugly insults at Aiken.) Clay said he wanted to be an example for children, then Simon followed with a snide remark, mocking, "This is for the children." But he admitted that Clay was growing on him—

what, like moss?

As a result, the competition didn't have the same added stress that Clay had of being beat up week after week by the guard. With every new performance, Aiken had to improve on the previous weeks SC quasi-betrayal in front of 20 to 30 million viewers, to try and dodge Simon's spiked whacking stick. The reality—Clay had to be stomped on because he was winning.

Another reality check. Remember that childhood game "LET'S PRETEND!" Let's pretend the night of the AI2 finals that every single vote was counted for both Clay and Ruben. Let's pretend all lines were available—no jams, no busy signals and no trying to fool Mother Nature. The CA fans consensus—there would have been no contest. Clay Aiken would have swept the competition.... The execs claimed on the afternoon of the finals the race was so close they could not even declare a winner. They later announced that 24 million votes were registered and Clay only lost by 134,400 votes. With the millions of Clay Aiken votes that were not counted—even Text Voters were blocked—imagine the results. I hear an Avalanche! Wait! Wait! Clay Fans screamed——Landslide!

Most media agreed.... Based on Clay Mania from the 2003 *American Idol* Tour, California Reporter Justin Chang wholeheartedly agreed when he wrote, "... if the outcome of '*American Idol*' were determined by the number of fans who showed up (for Clay) at Arrowhead Pond (Anaheim, California) for Sunday night's live concert, Clay Aiken, the show's runner-up, would have won by a landslide."

CHAPTER THIRTEEN

Come live in my heart, and pay no rent

Samuel Lover

DIANE SAWYER—
AN AVID CLAY AIKEN FAN

Screaming, shouting, waving posters, waiting for hours just for a peek—that kind of behavior is often the norm for those who process their love for Clay Holmes Aiken. However, his fans would beat his door down to be labeled one of "Clay's true loves," because he has a chosen few. Of course one of them is his mother and another love is D.S.

Clay loves her; he said it on National Television. "I love you Diane." When he said that every aiken heart in the country withered with envy. Not only does Clay Aiken love Diane Sawyer of *Good Morning America* fame—America loves her. She is one of the most respected women in television.

Diane was smitten with The Clay from the beginning. And

her adoration was displayed noticcably the day she was absent from *Good Morning America*. Her co-host Charles Gibson said she was at home in-mourning because of the approaching *American Idol* finals and she was afraid Clay might not win. The hype all week on all the Entertainment shows had been biased conspicuously toward Ruben.

Her concern was warranted. Clay didn't win the AI crown but he won the title of America's favorite. After the finals, *Good Morning America* invited Clay on their show—Diane's "admitted obsession" came in full view. When the segment began, the program aired Clay Aiken singing, "Sugar Pie Honey Bunch."

Bonnie Wallace

Diane melted and asked, "Who would that be Charlie?"

Charlie: "This guy, this guy is your heart throb."

Diane joked that she was accused of throwing preteens across the street so she could be on the front row when Clay Aiken came out.

Charlie: "He's going to be here! This brings to mind momentous meetings. There have been many in the past (for example) when: 'Stanley met Livingston,' 'Liz met Dick,' 'Harry met Sally,' and today 'Diane meets Clay'."

Charlie: "Well she's been a lot obsessed with him, championing him since the beginning."

Diane shared how she and Clay had e-mailed back and forth and that he mostly talked about his mother (laughter). She said,

"The story of my life."

DIANE then GOES OUTSIDE TO THE SCREAMING FANS and announces in her hand-held microphone: "At LONG LAST—CLAY AIKEN!" Clay walks onto the outside rostrum to massive screaming and applause. Diane and Clay embrace as Clay whispers—"Thank you so much. Thank you so much."

Signs, posters and banners are waving throughout the huge crowd. Young girls are dissolving and clutching his sleeve. Columns of middle-age women and some men have looks of halo'd worship. The crowd then calms down....

Diane: "You're so tall, I'm 5 foot 9 1/2, how tall are you?"

Clay: "I'm 6 foot 1."

The audience swoons....

Diane: "Wow, it's very hard to tell."

Clay: "When you stand by Ruben, you look short."

They talked about how dramatically his life has changed in just a few short months from his goal of working with Special Needs Kids. And how Clay and Ruben were the two least likely guys in America to end as the top two finalists because obviously the viewers didn't go with image this time, they went with talent. Clay also indicated he was there for all skinny white guys in America.

Diane: "Now let's talk about this transformation, in you over time."

Clay laughs: "What transformation, I've always looked like this?"

The program shows the clip of Clay when he first auditioned for *American Idol* with his bright red hair and those glasses.

Diane indicated that she missed his glasses and they talked about the effort it took to fix his spiky hair. Clay said it took a flat iron and a lot of hair spray and he usually has someone style it but when he does it he can do the front but the back of his hair is another story. Clay said that in the beginning he didn't trust anyone but he began to trust the AI hair stylists Dean Vandewist and Miles and those who helped choose his outfits when he performed on the show.

Clay talked about setting up a foundation and about his desire to bring attention to Autism awareness and individuals with disabilities.

Just before Clay performed "This Is The Night," he indicated how tired he was and confessed he really needed a break. At the end of the program Diane, Charlie and Clay stood outside and Diane laughed then gestured toward Charlie: "What's there to look forward to tomorrow—with you?"

Charlie: "... yah?" Everyone laughs....

Diane to Clay: "It is a breakneck pace."

Clay: "It is. It's amazing, I left Raleigh six months ago and nobody knew who I was. It's very hard to get used to."

Good Morning America has had Clay Aiken as a guest numerous times. GMA showcased Clay when he was presented his Double Platinum Award from Clive Davis for selling two million albums, "Measure Of A Man," its first week in release. Diane Sawyer also interviewed Clay on Primetime where she asked him many probing questions, especially about his biological father, Vernon Grissom. Other facets of his life were also brought to light. Clay Aiken also participated in GMA's Concert Series.

Blend Created By Bonnie Wallace

CHAPTER FOURTEEN

The bookshop has a thousand books
All colors, hues and tinges,
And every cover is a door,
That turns on magic hinges.

Nancy Byrd Turner

THE AMAZING INDOMINABLE
CLAY AIKEN FANS

Clay Aiken has many gifts: He's freckly handsome, he has a beautiful voice, an engaging personality, a life of decency, a smart encouraging mother, and the beat goes on.... However, he has another coveted gift—THE AMAZING INDOMITABLE CLAY AIKEN FANS. The world is in awe of the Claymates (they have many names). It is a jaw-dropping experience just watching them. Lucky Clay! Where did he find these Wonder Women and Men and their fleets? An observer cautioned, "Clay's Army is in place, and you don't mess around with them!" True statement.... When a soothsayer announced his New Year predictions that "Clay Aiken would be Out in 2004," his fans went ballistic with, "We'll show him who's out!" Clay Aiken's fans are absolute fanatics (Clanatics) who track his every move. And what's so refreshing—they are absolutely crazy for Clay Holmes Aiken.

Clay said during the finale of *American Idol*. "Whatever God wants me to have, it will happen." Well God has smiled on The Clay. As a result, many feel his mission has a responsibility. Such gifts are not bestowed to just anyone.

Bonnie Wallace

This endowment handed to Clay Aiken is the result of a promotional phenomenon. And the fee—NO CHARGE. Paula Abdul told the contestants, "*American Idol* offers the platform to set the blueprint for the rest of your career." *American Idol* has proved to be an unprecedented springboard that showcases talent to the world. The flipside—many great performers from assorted stages present themselves to audiences, but without that crucial exposure and a huge base of supportive fans their music goes unnoticed.

Clay Aiken is an extraordinary talent. However, his nonstop global marketing blitzkrieg offered at NO CHARGE is unheard of in today's cutthroat world of business. Corporate CEO's grovel for the powerful revenues that are handed to celebrity. Fans give idol-worship-labor that does not cost the famous a dime. Amazingly, the strategically calculated empowerments offered Clay Aiken are gifts from strangers who he will most likely never meet.

As a result, Mr. Aiken's Fans have bequeathed him with Super Stardom. First, they labored nonstop to assure that he was not voted off *American Idol*. Then these amazing puppeteers structured the chat rooms, who responded to their magical hand strings. The strategists announced their game plan and the volunteers deluged the boards and pledged their support. Many Clay fans admitted they had never taken part in Idol Worship, but they joined the brigade and as a result they carbon-copied the strategy and became duplicating machines for his success. Clay said, "It was a mathematical numbers game." Getting him in the top two was a big bucks mathematical numbers game, that didn't happen by chance.

Bonnie Wallace

Marketing is very costly. Many corporations wage millions of dollars to bet on mega returns. They contract top-notch marketing strategists. Some pay out-of-the-ballpark fees for celebrity endorsements. Most pay through the ceiling for product exposure.

Can you imagine what most would give, to work 5-6 months—then have the incredible global exposure that is generated from *American Idol*? And then have hundreds of thousands of volunteers, MARKET YOU (AT THEIR OWN

EXPENSE) TO GUARANTEE YOUR SUCCESS. I HAVE
BEEN IN MARKETING MOST OF MY ADULT LIFE AND
THIS IS ONE OF THE MOST AMAZING BESTOWAL I
HAVE EVER WITNESSED.

Clay's fans foot the bills to create expensive Websites.
They organize game plans, fan clubs, strategy teams, concert
and CD parties, and many support his foundations.
Reciprocation is never expected, so Aiken never receives a
monthly statement. These volunteers use their hard-earned
cash to buy multiple sets of CD's; in addition they spend count-
less hours designing T-Shirts and painting banners and posters.
They also travel hundreds of miles to attend concerts and never
expect anyone to chip in for gas.

Plus, the Claymates have cloned their own personal CLAY
AIKEN CORPORATION with him as CEO, and President.
They mirror his responsibilities, take charge of the Corporate
Policy's and Procedures, and monitor his daily job performance. The only embezzling concerns Mr. Aiken has are his
brigade would like to personally embezzle him which could be
a problem, because embezzlement practices have brought great
Corporations to their knees. Interestingly, CA will probably
never know the names or recognize the faces of those who run
his operation—they are the drill sergeants in mass—Clay's
Army. Regardless, they always show up for duty wearing
fatigues but are camouflaged in crowds, fighting to stand in the
front lines, just to see his face or by some miracle, get an auto-
graph. Most corporatists would give their eyeteeth to have this
task force in charge of their operations.

Turn the page and many Americans are on workaholic
treadmills. Most are so locked in debt and obligation with their
high mortgaged houses, high interest credit cards and over-
scheduled lives with their over-scheduled kids--as a result, they
have forgotten how to live. Plus most overworked wives and
mothers never cook. Many Americans have a junk food exis-
tence. The parents and their children are lo-nutritional-junk
food'd into stupors and exhaustion, so they depend of Big

Gulps of hourly caffeine to keep them going. Then there are the Single Parents (some of them merely children), who are trapped in uncalled-for-nightmares with uncalled-for-obligations. Then don't forget, the forgotten seniors—many live in isolated loneliness who are left to wait out there last years with silence and

Bonnie Wallace

neglect. What has happened to us?

In spite of our lifestyles or treadmills, Americans had an awakening Jolt! Our country was brought to its knees with the 9/11 disaster. It robbed the country of its safety net and bombed our sense of security. The Nation grieved with disbelief. The country is still on various shades of alert. Then after more than a year of mourning and rebuilding and trying to feel safe again— America declared war on Iraq. While our troops and insecurities were preparing for battle, *American Idol* blitzed its 2003 show on Fox. Talk about timing. Timing and Fox are King. And the Crown goes to: Simon Fuller of 19 TV Entertainment. This Entrepreneur of Talent has pulled off one of the greatest coops in television—in addition, he already had an commanding track record as long as a football field. However, producing *"Pop Idol"* and *"American Idol"* has not only quadrupled his noted brilliance, it has quadrupled his income.

Fuller's Reality Show offered some Tuesday and

Wednesday nights' diversion away from the bombings, tread-mills, obligations, and loneliness. Those who needed a break from the doldrums and despair put their doldrums on hold and tuned in. They watched and laughed and gasped then gave their applause, because they desperately needed a net of distraction. Then Clay Holmes Aiken walked on stage and sang to us—helping many to momentarily forget that the world was in crisis.

Blends Created By Bonnie Wallace

Oprah Winfrey said, "Clay has a spectacular voice that is music to our ears." The world needed something to soothe and to enliven the soul. The viewers caught a glimpse of someone so refreshing that it softened the reminder of alarm clocks, business demands, deadlines, nagging spouses, bawling kids, dirty dishes, and life's on overload. They sang along then started their own personal infatuation as they cheered boldly for him to win.

Whilst most were enchanted and echoing, "Boy that guy is amazing!" Aggressive fans from around the world were over-dosing—not on drugs but on OBC (Our Boy Clay). Armies were forming, yes in Iraq, plus organized teams were enlisting recruits for Clayton Holmes Aiken. As a result, *Google* and *Lycos* went on high alert with global websites pounding the Internet boards. An Affair was not only blooming, it was on fire. Miles of fans stood in line waving their posters, professing their undying love. For the first time in his life, Clay Aiken had no faults and Simon Cowell was the most despicable and most hated man on television.

Trackers were put in place to tract The Clay's every lip bite and every flutter of those delicious green eyes. Clanatics know with the click of a mouse his where-abouts and his what-abouts. The masses are programmed of when to vote for every poll and when and where to buy his CD's while monitoring his daily album sales. They know immediately, what critics praised "the wonder boy" and which ones slammed him. And the slammers get slammed big time from the entourage of e-mails directed at the negative big mouths. Not only that, most fans (from puberty to post menopause have designated themselves as his surrogate caretaker. (He coughed last night, I wonder if he is getting a cold-and heaven forbid, let us pray that he doesn't lose his voice.) Undoubtedly their prayers have been answered.

Clay's incredible fans—require very little of him. What they request is that he keeps singing; that he whispers an occa-sional, "Thank You," and that he always stays Clay Holmes Aiken, the true original—the guy they fell in love with. Where on Earth did he find these incredible people? Heaven inter-vened, most assuredly.

Blends Created By Bonnie Wallace

Gaye Deamer

CHAPTER FIFTEEN

Randy Jackson: "What was the most memorable moment of your Idol experience?"

Clay: "... going home and singing for my hometown on the tour and... being introduced for the first time in Raleigh.... The support that came out of that city was unbelievable, unexpected, and overwhelming."

THE AMERICAN IDOL TOUR—
THE WINNER IS CROWNED

The AI 2003 Tour attracted impressive crowds. Kellogg's was its sponsor—namely, the *"Pop Tart American Idol Tour."* Regardless, the critics kept their computers smokin'. Many critics gave favorable reviews but an equal number slammed it as a karaoke substitute. However, almost every critic praised Clay Aiken's showmanship that dominated the tour coupled with his panoply of zealous fans.

Apart from the lopsided reviews, the 2003 AI Tour was a

"money machine" for Simon Fuller's 19 Entertainment. The debut *"American Idol"* tour in 2002, highlighting the 10 finalists, reportedly grossed $8.1 million and sold about 258,500 tickets to 30 shows. The 2003 tour, featuring nine finalists nearly doubled that take, bringing in almost $16 million with 411,000 attending 39 shows. The 2004 tour performed in over 50 cities, some in smaller venues. An impressive feat, considering the background and experience of the performing contestants—almost all are homespun kids. The 2003 tour of mostly inexperienced entertainers carried a national tour that rallied hysteria around the country. Amazing when you think about it! No wonder Fuller has been so supportive of Clay Aiken because most of the ado was "Aiken for Clay."

Another ace for the *American Idol* Tour—the show was the only teen-slanted 2003 draw in the summer's concert series. Melissa Ruggeiri reporting by phone with Gary Bongiovanni, editor of *Pollstar*, said "The first 11 cities they had received data on, they were filling about 10,000 seats per night." However, some cities filled over 13,000 to 14,000 seats depending on the size of the venue.... Trade magazine Pollstar reported that the first show at Xcel Energy Center in St. Paul, Minn., grossed nearly $436,000 for the night, filling 10,817 of the 13,056 seats with reasonable ticket prices ranging from $26.50 to $46.50 each. When one considers that many-noted entertainer's tickets are double, triple, or even quadruple those prices; the tour was a smashing success....

As mentioned, only nine *American Idol* finalists participated beginning (July 8, 2003) at the Xcel Energy Center in St. Paul, Minnesota. The 39-non-stop, city-to-city concerts continued through (August 31, 2003) ending with their last performance in Anaheim, California at the Arrowhead Pond. Clay Aiken and Ruben Studdard—whose first singles debuted at Numbers One and Two, respectively, on the Billboard Hot 100 chart—were the headliners, which also features 3rd Runner-up, Kimberly Locke then Carmen Rasmussen, Trenyce, Rickey Smith, Julia DeMato, Kimberly Caldwell, and Charles Grigsby.

A 10th *American Idol* contestant, Joshua Gracin was not able to participate due to military commitments with the U.S. Marine Corps.

Trenyce reported the *American Idol* entourage traveled in four touring buses (*CNN* reported three.) However, they slept on the buses when the performing cities were close—like from Birmingham, Alabama to Memphis, Tennessee. Other nights they stayed in hotels across the country. Contestants indicated a lot of time was spent packing and unpacking. Ruben said, "We are in the business of heavenly comfort so we love the Westin Hotels—we love them!" However, other hotels were also reserved for the state-to-state extravaganzas. The contestants accommodated two buses.... Clay, Ruben, Carmen and Kimberly Locke stayed together in one bus, while Julie, Kim Caldwell, Trynece, Rickey and Charles, rode in the second one.

Bonnie Wallace

Providence Journal's Andy Smith interviewed Kimberly Locke during the tour. Kimberly who lived in Nashville Tennessee started her *American Idol* climb with chock-full curly hair and glasses. She was an administrative assistant planning to enter law school before her friends and co-workers encouraged her to audition. She later became serious competition for Clay and Ruben being voted to the top final three. Locke pointed out for the "Pop Tart Idol Tour," the singers were able to choose their own songs and they had a live band rather than the show's pre-recorded accompaniments. The tour was also a drastic, yet refreshing change from the *American Idol* weekly show. The nine contestants finally exhaled and vented some frustrations after the competition ended. They told of the tremendous pressure they were under while competing. Toward the end they were all exhausted. Clay said, "If they wake me up to do one more thing, I am going to scream." The other contestants echoed his frustrations.

Kimberly Locke said, "We came from ordinary lives, and suddenly you are on everybody's TV. Week after week you are under such scrutiny." The other contestants agreed the greatest pressure was every few days they had to learn a new genus of songs. One week it was "Songs from a Movie," and the next week it was "Country Rock," so they had to mentally shift gears and get psyched up week after week for an entirely new menu of performance. They had three days to pick a song, arrange it, learn it, rehearse it, hopefully discover the meaning of the song, then deliver a performance so impressive they would not get voted off. Plus, they had to practice group songs for that week and also work on a completely different theme for the week ahead. Then the finalists were constantly thrust in front of the media, they attended meetings with Music executives, went to Movie Premiers, signed autographs and the obligations were endless. The judges qualified the contestants have to be put through the *American Idol* process not only for AI to find the best performers but to help the winners deal with the aftermath of Fame.

Even though touring included a hectic schedule; a major boon was they didn't have to compete against each other. Another biggie—Simon's mouth was in another corner of the Country writing his book—another avenue he could use to flame his well-calculated celebrity.

However, Cowell continued his degradation of the 2nd Runner-up, Clay Aiken. Locke said. "Sometimes I wanted to smack him," Clay said Simon was never nice to him and six months after the competition when Clay had breaking record sales Clay confirmed that Simon still treats him as he always did. Clay had a face-to-face talk with Simon after the competition and reiterated that Cowell's brutal comments still affected him. Simon countered, "Get Over It!" One critic said there has to be some reverse psychology going on with the Simon verses Aiken. Others indicated there's no psychology—Simon is Simon.

Regardless, the nine touring contestants were letting off steam and were having a ball as they traveled from venue to venue. Clay, Ruben, Carmen, Trenyce, Julie and Rickey appeared on Canada AM while doing their show in Toronto (their 11th AI Pop Tart Show). They talked nonstop about the "good, the bad and the ugly" of touring and living on the buses. The Host Seamus, laughed and said the talk fest with the AI group was one of the toughest interviews he had ever done. If you watched it, it was obvious why, because Seamus could not get a word in edge-wise. The AI entertainers all interrupted each other and laughed so much he could not get control of the group. It was apparent they were having a great time performing, even though it was a grueling schedule.

Carmen chimed, "If you need to know anything about the 'touring show' just ask me?" But Carmen's "just ask me" was drowned because everyone in the AI Group were so chatty and in high spirits very little could be asked or answered. However, during the interview there were a few discernible tidbits shared about the tour and the bus....

There were difficulties living on the road. The buses were comfortable but it wasn't easy to sleep. Clay said when the bus went around a corner everyone rolled from side to side in their bunks. Rickey added when they sat up in the bunks they bumped their heads. But Ruben countered that he could sit up without bumping his head, and pointed out that nobody in his bus had any complaints. It was also pointed out if you were on the top bunk you could fall off. Trenyce said the buses were not uncomfortable per sey, it was just really hard to go to bed. She said she didn't go to bed unless she was dead tired because it was like sleeping in a coffin. Julie indicated she was so tired every night she would just pass out. The touring Clan said they slept until 2 o'clock the next day because after each show they didn't crash because they were too hyper.

Seamus asked African-American Rickey, "Do you see faces when you look in the audience or are they all black?" The AI Group cracked up—Rickey said they see individual faces but when the lights go out all the faces look black. During an AI video segment, again happy-go-lucky Rickey was asked what was the very worst thing the contestants did on the bus. Rickey waved his hand in front of his face and said "When people fart," it was awful because there was nowhere to escape.

During the entire *American Idol* experience including the tour, the contestants virtually lived in each other's back pockets. Clay said it would have been really difficult if they weren't such close friends. He said, "After you've been together for nine months and you have gone through all the good stuff, the bad stuff and the hard stuff, you learn to work together as a team—you can't fake it. And because they work together they are like a tight family."

Canada AM host Seamus was kind. He indicated that the *American Idol* performers were so comfortable with each other that they actually finish each other's sentences.

Right is the eternal sun;
the world cannot delay its coming

Wendell Phillips

THE AMERICAN IDOL TOUR mini REVIEWS:

ST. PAUL STAR TRIBUNE— "Aiken.... showed true star quality. Not only was he a natural onstage, conversing with confidence and glee, but he also commanded the stage.... He can match Manilow for sentiment and style, but he has a much more impressive voice.... And when he moved away from the mike stand and crouched for emphasis, the crowd went wild."

CHICAGO TRIBUNE—"'*American Idol* II' offered something its predecessor didn't have: character. This year's...Idols, Ruben Studdard and Clay Aiken, have rich, soulful voices, unlike last year's square pegs. If there was a winner of this perpetual competition, it was Aiken...only Aiken has the natural charm to do justice to the 'Idol' mantle. Expect him to steal your heart."

CINCINATI ENQUIRER— "Other 'Idols' perform admirably but runner-up on top Clay Aiken may not be the *American Idol*, but he is America's sweetheart, hands down. He owned the audience at U.S. Bank Arena before ever stepping on the stage Sunday night as part of 'American Idols Live.'"

MTV NEWS—"Not only is 'Idol' runner-up Clay Aiken beating the champ on the Billboard singles charts, but on the fifth stop of the "Idol" summer tour, the spiky-haired'crooner proved that he's winning the battle for the hearts and minds of "Idol" fans across the country."

INDIANAPOLIS STAR REVIEW— "His (Clay's) hot streak continued...where he was quicker with a quip and stronger with a lyric. After an audience member tossed something past Aiken's face...the singer responded with deadpan self-deprecation: 'If those are somebody's panties, I'm out of here'...."

WILKES-BARRE TIMES LEADER— "The arrival of Clay Aiken brought the house down with Beatle mania-type shrieks... With Aiken, the comparisons are true: the kid is a young Barry Manilow, right down to the body language. And like Manilow, he can really sing."

BUFFALO NEWS— "They were clearly 'Aiken for Clay.' His performance left no doubt as to why. He hits the high notes, charms the crowd, and has a surprisingly powerful stage presence. The audience could hardly catch a glimpse of Aiken without bursting into deafening screams...."

DAILY GAZETTE— (Upstate NY) "Aiken is a passionate, expressive singer, and he's got a long prosperous career ahead if his performance Monday night is any indication. Everything he sang ... was impressive. It was no surprise that the crowd, which was heavily female, went nuts for this guy. Clay Aiken has got what it takes to go the distance."

CHART ATTACH TORONTO— "One thing was clear after seeing these kids play live - while Ruben Studdard was likely voted *American Idol* fair and square, the people's Idol is, without a doubt Clay Aiken."

SACTICKET— "Clay Aiken is the '*American Idol*.' Sure, Ruben Studdard ...won the '*American Idol*' title in May. That's just a technicality. Judging by the scream-athon that greeted Aiken at Thursday night's American Idols Live! Show at Arco Arena, he's eclipsed the competition."

CLEVELAND BEAKON JOURNAL— "Aiken is no runner-up with CSU crowd. Clay Aiken may not have won the competition but he has won the hearts of millions of females...every other time he took the stage—he was greeted by screams that would make a family of banshees jealous."

BOSTON HERALD— "But while that show...felt distinctly like a live version of the TV series, this felt more like a concert. That's probably due to the overall level of talent this time around.... With a powerful voice that belies his slight stature, Aiken out sang everyone."

WASHINGTON POST— "It was runner-up Clay Aiken, a lanky Southerner with an epic voice and flirty ways.... From the number of homemade T-shirts, signs and earsplitting screams that erupted at his slightest peep, Aiken was the night's winner, if not the shows."

ALBANY TIMES UNION— "Clay Aiken, the most accomplished performer and most likely to have a long career...Aiken's voice had too few chances to go on and on... his new single, 'Invisible,' is undistinguished FM Lite—but the guy's got immense talent and he's developed significant charisma."

THE DAILY GAZETTE (NY)— "Aiken is a passionate, expressive singer, and he's got a long prosperous career ahead.... Everything he sang... was impressive. It was no surprise that the crowd, which was heavily female, went nuts for this guy. Clay Aiken has got what it takes to go the distance."

PROVIDENCE JOURNAL— "Idol audience is like putty in Clay Aiken's hands. There were lots of families... and many fans waved signs supporting a favorite Idol, most often Clay Aiken, the skinny guy with the big pipes.... Sure enough, AIKEN showed the most talent and stage presence..."

RICHMOND TIMES DISPATCH— "Before Aiken even nudged a toe onstage, every videotaped glimpse of him elicited shrieks of lust and devotion from the audience of about 8,000.... Many say....Broadway would be lucky to have him."

RALEIGH NEWS OBSERVER—.... Aiken made the dramatic entrance.... When he finished, he stood silently... as the audience screamed its love.... "Thank you so much," he said, appearing to tear up. "There's no place like home".... Before singing "Invisible".... he again became emotional, introducing his mom and showing his appreciation for the crowd. "I would never be able in a thousand years to thank you for what you've done for me."

MIAMI HERALD— "If the decibel level on the applause meter could be converted into CD sales, runner-up and clear fan favorite Clay Aiken could retire a wealthy man about now. This makes sense, too. Clay is Idol's find. He's the one with the most talent, the surest voice, the most presence."

PALM BEACH POST— "Aiken emerged as the true joy of the night.... He can deliver a simple pop song with unbridled gusto.... Think Celine Dion in her best moments. But he does it without a trace of ego and with a genuine sense of gratitude.... But Aiken's talent has been well-heralded...."

GO MEMPHIS— "The Memphis crowd let it be known who they came to see, though, as they roared their loudest when Aiken's video montage came up and his voice echoed throughout 'The Pyramid' as he sang the ballad This is the Night."

THE DESERET NEWS—Salt Lake City— "It may have been Carmen Rasmussen's homecoming, but it was Clay Aiken's show when 'American Idols Live' hit the Delta Center on Saturday night.... There was no doubt the same crowd would have voted runner-up Aiken the top spot... judging by the screaming — which began when Clay appeared in video clips...."

SALT LAKE TRIBUNE— "Aiken was clearly the crowd favorite during the show."

SEATTLE TIMES— "Runner-up Clay steals spotlight in *'American Idol'* concert.... The skinny, spiky-haired runner-up...elicited the loudest screams when he appeared onstage.... Aiken, 24, commanded the stage with the practiced ease of a talk-show host....Then he sang - and the boy can sing - and the crowd screamed, impossibly, louder."

ORANGE COUNTY REGISTER—"They came screaming for Clay.... More beneficial to his rising popularity... his dramatic voice wrapped in boy-next-door looks - is the fact that he's virtually alone in a field of young trade-pop stars. His appealing demeanor and ability to handle mid tempo mainstream...bodes well for his future."

 LA TIMES— "Though he finished second.... Akin was clearly the star attraction...it was Aiken who turned the Pond into the House of Clay.... Aiken eased through his numbers with effortless poise and charisma.... it was clear from the resounding reaction to Aiken's every move who will likely come out as the real winner..."

American Idol 2 Touring Schedule

Date   City/State   Venue

7-08-03 - ST. PAUL, MN - Xcel Energy Center
7-09-03 - CHICAGO, IL - United Center
7-11-03 - COLUMBUS, OH - Nationwide Arena
7-12-03 - INDIANAPOLIS, IN - Conseco Fieldhouse
7-13-03 - CINCINNATI, OH - US Bank Arena
7-15-03 - PITTSBURGH, PA - Mellon Arena
7-16-03 - WILKES-BARRE, PA - First Union Arena
7-18-03 - HARTFORD, CT - Hartford Civic Center
7-19-03 - BUFFALO, NY - HSBC Arena
7-20-03 - DETROIT, MI - Joe Louis Arena

7-22-03 - TORONTO, ONTARIO - Air Canada
7-23-03 - CLEVELAND, OH - Convocation Center
7-25-03 - WORCESTER, MA - Centrum Center
7-27-03 - PHILADELPHIA, PA - First Union Center
7-28-03 - WASHINGTON, DC - MCI Center
7-30-03 - EAST RUTHERFORD, NJ - Continental
7-31-03 - UNIONDALE, NY - Nassau Coliseum
8-02-03 - PROVIDENCE, RI - Dunkin Donuts Center
8-04-03 - ALBANY, NY - Pepsi Arena
8-05-03 - RICHMOND, VA - Richmond Coliseum
8-06-03 - RALEIGH, NC - RBC Center
8-08-03 - CHARLOTTE, NC - Charlotte Coliseum
8-09-03 - ATLANTA, GA - Philips Arena
8-10-03 - ORLANDO, FL - TD Waterhouse Center
8-12-03 - FT. LAUDERDALE, FL - Office Depot Center
8-13-03 - TAMPA, FL - St. Pete Times Forum
8-15-03 - BIRMINGHAM, AL - BJCC Arena
8-16-03 - MEMPHIS, TN - Pyramid Center
8-17-03 - ST. LOUIS, MO - Savvis Center
8-19-03 - DALLAS, TX - American Airlines Center
8-20-03 - HOUSTON, TX - Compaq Center
8-21-03 - OKLAHOMA CITY, OK -Oklahoma Ford Cemter
8-23-03 - SALT LAKE CITY, UT -Delta Center
8-24-03 - BOISE, ID - The Pavilion
8-26-03 - SEATTLE, WA - Key Arena
8-27-03 - PORTLAND, OR - Rose Garden
8-28-03 - SACRAMENTO, CA - Arco Arena
8-30-03 - SAN JOSE, CA - HP Pavilion
8-31-03 - ANAHEIM, CA - Arrowhead Pond

CHAPTER SIXTEEN

American celebrities have an amazing amount of influence on the way America thinks, feels, and acts. I think that such an influence should be used in the most positive way possible.

Clay Aiken

THE CLAY AIKEN-KELLY CLARKSTON INDEPENDENT TOUR

MTV—Clay Aiken, Kelly Clarkson Plan Joint Headlining Tour...."We are thrilled about sharing the stage for this momentous next step in both of our careers," Aiken continued, "...he was proud to be associated with the show and fellow contestants like Clarkson.... And hopefully we'll continue to be someone (the audience) can relate to."

The Independent Tour was a smashing success with an 84.57% capacity crowd.

Number of Shows: 30

Total Gross: $11,203,887
Average Gross: $373,463

Total Attendance: 249,790
Average Attendance: 8326
Average Capacity: 9846
% Capacity: 84.57%

Top Venue Attendance/Ticket Sales

Raleigh: 13,538 ($586,230)
Nassau (LI): 12,501 ($565,19)
DC: 10,627 ($458,12)
Worcester: 10,408 ($448,170)
St. Paul: 10,238 ($464,227)
Chicago: 10,002 ($436,250)

Soldout: 5
Raleigh
Winston-Salem
Worcester
Grand Prairie
St. Paul

Blends Created By Bonnie Wallace

Clay/Kelly Tour Schedule - Date/City/Venue

Feb. 24: Charlotte, NC - Charlotte Coliseum
Feb. 25: Duluth, GA - Gwinnett Center
Feb. 27: Tampa, FL - St. Pete Times Forum
Feb. 28: Miami, FL - American Airlines Arena
Mar. 01: Raleigh, NC - RBC Center
Mar. 02: Philadelphia, PA - Liacouras Center
Mar. 04: Long Island, NY - Nassau Coliseum
Mar. 05: Washington, DC - MCI Center
Mar. 07: Wilkes Barre, PA - Wachovia Arena
Mar. 08: Worcester, MA - Centrum Center
Mar. 10: Columbus, OH - Schottenstein Center
Mar. 11: Detroit, MI - Joe Louis Arena
Mar. 13 : Winston-Salem, - NC LJVM Coliseum
Mar. 19 : Grand Prairie, - TX Next Stage
Mar. 21 : St. Louis, MO - Savvis Center
Mar. 22 : Chicago, IL - United Center
Mar. 24 : Omaha, NE - Qwest Center
Mar. 26 : Salt Lake City, - UT Delta Center or "E" Center
Mar. 27 : Las Vegas, NV - Thomas & Mack
Mar. 30 : San Diego, CA - Cox Arena
Mar. 31 : Sacramento, - CA ARCO Arena
Apr. 02 : Glendale, AZ - Glendale Arena
Apr. 03 : Anaheim, CA - Arrowhead Pond
Apr. 05 : Los Angeles, CA - Staples Center
Apr. 06 : San Jose, CA - HP Pavilion
Apr. 08 : Seattle, WA - Key Arena
Apr. 09 : Spokane, WA - Spokane Arena
Apr. 13 : Denver, CO - Pepsi Center
Apr. 15 : Kansas City, MO - Kemper Arena
Apr. 16 : St. Paul, MN - Xcel Energy Center

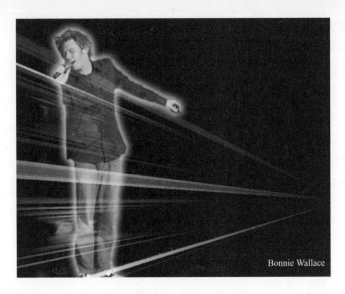

Bonnie Wallace

INDEPENDENT TOUR MINI REVIEWS:

TIME— "Lob it all his way - the Howdy Doody look-alike jokes, the is-he-or-isn't-he quips... because, as he prepares for his first major concert tour on his own, fresh off appearances...one thing is clear.... He is the guy who really won the last *American Idol*."

WCNC— "... all eyes were on Aiken Tuesday night at the Charlotte Coliseum for the first night of a 32 city concert tour with '*American Idol*' winner Kelly Clarkson."

CHARLOTTE OBSERVER— "When Aiken sang... 'When you say you love me do you mean it,' he was met with deafening cheers. Aiken played up his heartthrob image by pulling on his button-down shirt as if he'd tear it off during his current hit 'Invisible'."

TAMPA TRIBUNE— "If crowd reaction is any measure of who is the real '*American Idol*,' give the crown to Clay Aiken. The spiked-hair crooner... was greeted with screams from adoring fans.... The audience of 10,823 was predominantly female... from grandmothers to preteens.... Aiken clearly was the crowd favorite."

ST. PETE TIMES— "Aiken ran... with the show, dramatically appearing from the back of the arena to the... arousing the crowd.... All night, he was charismatic and assured. Unlike Clarkson, he seemed completely at home onstage.... ...he seemed every inch the star.

Bonnie Wallace

SUN SENTINAL REVIEW— "'I think he is the right person at the right time,' says Fran Skinner—Lewis, who runs the Bubel/Aiken Foundation.... 'what you're finding is that there has been a need... for a role model who is a real role model, not a manufactured role model.'"

PALM BEACH POST— "...his affection for his fan base is clearly genuine. And of the thousands in the audience, the Aiken contingent — or 'Claymates' — was the loudest."

MIAMI HERALD REVIEW— "The performance Saturday night showed that the poised, charismatic and confident Aiken can handle more than the unchallenging, overproduced pop mush of 'The Way' and 'When You Say You Love Me'...."

SUN SENTINEL— "... the self—professed nerd's special-ty is a squeaky-clean sincerity. With his loose-limbed walk, jacket-and-jeans... and half-shy stage moves... it's impossible not to be won over by him. The average member of his audience (would) like to have him for a son-in-law."

BEAVERS ON IDOL— "It may have been billed as the Kelly Clarkson/Clay Aiken Independent Tour but to the sold out crowd at the RBC Center in Raleigh on Monday night it was 'The Clay Aiken Show' with two opening acts."

NEWS OBSERVER— "... The sold-out, overwhelmingly female crowd went completely bonkers. This was a show where you could sense the audience as a living, breathing organism, and it reacted with hysteria to... the opening acts' references to Aiken, or... anything he did onstage."

WRAL— "Ginger Strazzulla, 70, of Boston, and her niece, Karlyn Fuller (said) '... He is the type of voice for every gen-eration.' Strazzulla said. '...he is a role model for the younger people of today. It is so refreshing to listen to him and not have to turn my ears away....'"

FOXES ON IDOL— "Kelly and Clay prove that you don't need pyrotechnics and a dance line to entertain. ... they rely on their vocals, which is rather refreshing.... (Clay and Kelly) both put their all into their show and it's a pleasure to see a two hour show of talent over production."

PHILADELPHIA INQUIRER— "The ladies began to scream as Aiken emerged from the back of the hall, singing Mr. Mister's 1985 hit 'Kyrie' as he walked through the audience. And they continued to scream all the way through his final number and latest single, 'The Way.'"

NEW YORK POST— "There's never been a question whether or not Aiken can sing. What this concert showed was that, when placed under the lights on a concert stage, the lanky Southerner is an entertainer. Wearing jeans, a rugby shirt and a sports coat, Aiken was completely unpretentious."

NEW YORK NEWSDAY— *"American Idol* groomed Aiken and Clarkson to resemble other successful pop stars... hence, they resemble each other. Though one is male, the other female, they can be described with the same few words: Young, talented, likable."

WASHINGTON POST— " Fans, (were) a mix of screaming teens and equally ecstatic middle-aged women.... he paused to talk to a fan's friend on her cell phone — coaching the hysterical woman to 'breathe, honey, breathe' — his geeky grin sent the crowd into further delirium."

WILKES-BARRE TWP— "...Aiken was better.... The reason...he embraces the songs. ... he truly... captures the feelings of the songs' lyrics, and... makes them his own.... There's also innocence to Aiken... his fame is still new... and... he's excited... and appreciative of it. That, too, makes him an engaging entertainer."

BOSTON GLOBE— "The evening was all about Aiken.... Prepubescent girls, and some... on the shadier side of adolescence whooped and hollered for Aiken.... Accompanied by two Studdard-size guards, Aiken entered the arena ...as if he were a conquering hero, singing 'Kyrie...'"

BOSTON HERALD— "(Clay's) effortless banter with the crowd was delightful. He... saw a 5-year-old girl with a sign... 'Clay, can I sing with you?' he brought her on stage... (she) knew all the words to 'When You Say You Love Me.' ...the Raleigh, N.C., native seemed to be having a blast on stage."

THE TELEGRAM— "At a time when the school of pop is awash with ne'er-do-wells and harlots, Aiken & Clarkson present themselves as safe alternatives. And that warm, cushy feeling was embraced by a near-sellout house."

THE TELEGRAPH— "Talk about meteoric rises: Aiken's spiky... head must be spinning.... If there is one thing better than his voice, it's his stage presence. This guy... never broke a sweat... he was so comfortable with the screaming throngs of estrogen-emitting females."

COLUMBUS DISPATCH— "Idol worship was on display... when a force named Clay Aiken rolled into town .... Females from toddlers to middle-aged mothers sported Aiken T-shirts, painted his name across their faces and carried banners with pictures of the *American Idol* runner-up turned international phenomenon."

THE FLINT JOURNAL— "If Aiken's easygoing charms... and obvious popularity with the mostly female crowd were any indication, he doesn't have to play second fiddle to anyone anymore.... it ... from little girls to their grandmas, was mostly there to see him."

WINSTON-SALEM REVIEW— "One woman... had a sign for every... Aiken song... he asked her.... 'do you know what I'm singing next? If you pick the correct one, you can come backstage.... Don't cheat now! .... y'all that have seen the show 15 times can't help her'.... the woman responded... Aiken asked if she got help. 'You did? Well... you get to come backstage... for being honest.'"

THE DALLAS MORNING NEWS— "Remember that goofball... the one who sang 'Grease' wearing a red-leather jacket while displaying an appalling lack of rhythm? He's gone, replaced by an ultra-confident, laid-back, rhythmically competent, bedroom-eyed hunk. It's official: Clay is sexy."

THE STAR-TELEGRAM— "It's about time that mothers and daughters were able to find a boy they can agree on. Judging from the full house at Nokia Live on Friday night, that time has come, and that boy is the wholesome Southerner Clay Aiken."

ST. LOUIS DISPATCH— "...it was clear whom the crowd really had come to hear. They were on their feet from the opening note.... With self-effacing humor, some simple but playful dance steps and a boatload of personality, Aiken cherry-picked his CD..."

CHICAGO TRIBUNE— "*American Idol* judge Simon Cowell has an endless supply of snarky quips and wry put-downs, (with) one dismissal... 'You've got talent,' he generally begins, before dropping the ax. 'But we're looking for a star'.... The... show ... has only produced one real star: Clay Aiken."

CHICAGO SUN-TIMES— "The two idols have been taking turns closing the show, and on this night it was Aiken who opened for Clarkson.... With his shock of red hair and big smile, it was hard not to warm up to Aiken, who happily cackled at his own jokes and make fun of his onstage clumsi-ness."

OMAHA WORLD HERALD— "Problems? So much bass that the seats literally shook, especially during Clarkson's set. So much over-miking that some of Aiken's crystal-clear high notes... sounded as if he were singing on helium. Nonetheless, the audience had a great time...."

THE DAILY HERALD— "All the Clay-mates were out in force at the Delta Center on Friday night to see '*American Idol*' talents, Clay Aiken and Kelly Clarkson....Aiken... gave a shout-out to Utah's Carmen Rasmussen, who was in the audience, during his charming hour long set....Aiken's fun personality made the show entertaining...."

DESERET NEWS— "Aiken... was full of charm, and he connected with the audience.... Smartly dressed in an untucked blue shirt, blue necktie and khaki slacks, Aiken with his boyish smile slid into "Perfect Day'.... But (Clarkston's)... chunky wardrobe, complete with stiletto heels, was a bit much."

SACRAMENTO REVIEW— "The Clay Nation was aching for Aiken.... The usual puns aside, people love Clay Aiken. Love is a strong word.... Likewise, there was a palpable shock when the innocent Aiken delivered a pelvic thrust when dancing with a backup singer during... 'When Doves Cry.'"

GLENDALE REVIEW— "Arizona's chapter of 'Claymates' was out in full force... to witness... unlikely sex symbol, Clay Aiken deliver a wholesome, charming... vocally impressive set.... From toddlers to grandmas and grandpas, the crowd went into a frenzy as Aiken opened the show...."

GET OUT Magazine— "(Clay) seemed comfortably at ease onstage, acknowledging the signs of fans including one that read, 'Save a marriage - hug my wife!' which he did. His south-ern drawl and unassuming nature seemed to connect with the crowd."

CONTRA COSTA TIMES— "Maybe it was the woman... who said 'American Idol' got her through a long hospital stay...(or) the seven giddy middle-aged women...from the same office clad in Clay Aiken T-shirts. Or... all those old ladies running around in "Grandmas for Clay" shirts...yet there's... no preparing a cynic for the non-threatening, charm machine that is Clay Aiken"

LA TIMES— "It's a dream team for fans.... The Pond audience wasn't one to sit back and clap politely. They screamed and shouted and waved signs that said such things as 'Taken With Aiken' and 'Kelly Rocks.'"

ORANGE COUNTYY REGISTER— "So thank whatever musical gods... to help pop fans save face... to discover Kelly Clarkson and Clay Aiken. (They) proved repeatedly during their sets Saturday night at Arrowhead Pond of Anaheim, they are powerhouse voices who deserve their devoted followings. "

NORTH COUNTY TIMES— "The tousle-haired, freckled Aiken... in a... midnight blue... shirt, tie and his... ('What Would Jesus Do') bracelet... with his flawless pale skin, bright green eyes, pearly smile and no makeup. The once-wholesome-looking Clarkson had...dark makeup, tattoos, nose stud, tight black tank top... bra straps...torn jeans, bare feet and a few more pounds...."

SAN HOSE MERCURY— "Kelly Clarkson and Clay Aiken shared a concert stage Tuesday night, but it was Aiken who shone like the true pop star. Just the mere glimpse of Aiken who's co-headlining a national concert tour with first-season *American Idol* winner Clarkson — sent the audience into a frenzy at the HP Pavilion in San Jose."

SAN FRANCISCO CHRONICLE— "The *American Idol* runner-up also has a glorious set of pipes and among the worst taste of any singer this side of Engelbert Humperdinck, although that jacket with the stripes across the back was so bad, somebody else must have told him to wear it."

SEATTLE POST— "Aiken was charming and animated (with) such favorites as 'I Will Carry You,' 'Measure of a Man' and 'The Way.' Though he doesn't push the creative envelope of popular music, the 25-year-old from Raleigh, N.C., is a natural talent with a powerful voice and a flair for engaging his fans."

SEATTLE TIMES— "Without question, Aiken seemed to be the one most came to see... at Key Arena. His fans are notoriously loyal, known in some circles as 'Claymates,' and reflect a true cross-section of America: from children to tweens and teens, parents and grandparents, students and professionals."

SPOKESMAN-REVIEW— "One area where Aiken has grown... is in his showmanship. While Aiken has a corny appeal... he seemed more comfortable... in his own skin. Even with an apparent broken foot from tripping during his show in Seattle, Aiken limped around the stage, charming the crowd between songs."

KANSAS CITY STAR— "The ostensibly sincere performer thanked his fans for their support, and dedicated the love song 'The Way' to the loyal crowd sporting the 'Clay Mates' T-shirts all around him."

ST. PAUL STAR TRIBUNE- "Even Clarkson knows that in the year since she released her debut album, Aiken has eclipsed her in popularity.... The special education teacher from Raleigh, N.C., has an astoundingly faithful following for a new artist, and the power-pop ballads he leans on play to his strengths."

ROCKY MOUNTAIN REVIEW— "There was this weird feeling of *dey ja^ vu* at the Aiken-Clarkson concert... and then it struck you... this is what concerts used to be like. Live singing, performers interacting with the fans. And just as important, a sense of audience identification with the artist."

CHAPTER SEVENTEEN

Oprah Winfrey is the richest woman in the world.
She is the only self-made (female) billionaire on the planet.
Oprah has given away over $50 million of her personal
fortune to support humanitarian causes.

OPRAH WINFREY—AN AMERICAN ICON

Clay Aiken was asked, "Who is your favorite celebrity?."
He unequivocally said "Oprah"—with good reason. And the
world agrees. How can anyone not admire the woman; the talk
show host, the humanitarian and the list could be another book-
on the poetry of her life.

Avid fans of Winfrey have backpacked the torrid mountains
she has climbed and have been in awe of what she has over-
come with her pure unadulterated grit and perseverance. The
viewers pay attention and applaud her verve—she gives such
hope to others as her admirers have watched her confront and
conquer her past. Oprah has challenged and reconciled a dysfunctional upbringing. She has defied a carnivorous childhood
of sexual abuse and the traumas of growing up in an environment of depravation and misconduct. Let's pause— she doesn't

defy the dysfunction, she has come face to face with it—worked her way through the debris and refused to let the terror engulf whom she was destined to be—the remarkable Oprah Winfrey. I am sure she is still addressing her former milieu that could have stolen the best of her life, but she somehow incarcerates the memories of adolescent intruders and in every season of her life, she captures greater acclaim.

Let's compare Oprah to those who achieve and sustain celebrity by humiliating others. Oprah Winfrey's earlier programs were caught up in that genre of shock and sensationalism—engaging in the show ship of individuals and families' dysfunctional display. A lot of daytime and nighttime talk entertainment has gravitated to baseness—many programmers still offer sleaze as their daily entre of carte du jour. As a result, Oprah took a brave stance when she witnessed the carnage of her program's expose—after a wife was shown an affair of her adulterous husband on Winfrey's national television show. The wife was devastated. Oprah was so distraught when she examined the damage, she proclaimed, "That will never happen again on my show!" She made a turn-about-face and changed the entire blueprint of her program. She said, "I am guided by the vision of what I believe this show can be." The new format was to uplift, enlighten, encourage and entertain. She was warned that her viewing audience could be turned off and her ratings could plummet. Oprah would not relent. She took the position and went for a higher ground and it paid off. Then later, she has added a new mission statement for *The Oprah Winfrey Show,* "To use television to transform people's lives, to make viewers see themselves differently and to bring happiness and a sense of fulfillment into every home." And since she turned 50 years old she has even set new goals and commitments to making the world a better place. Yes, Oprah Winfrey is one of a kind. She is a legend of hope. She is an American Icon.

HER LIFE OF ACHIEVEMENT IS UNPRECEDENTED

Her Midas Touch is from gut-wrenching effort. And she uses her influence for the good of mankind. Let's examine what this remarkable lady has accomplished. There is no other woman (or man) who has amassed this caliber of renown and there is no one who can claim this level of achievement. Her accomplishments are so massive, one questions ownership. If you want to venture through her book without a binding, "Go to her Website" and read the story of her life. Reading what she has accomplished, inspires the reader to make a pledge to offer some contributions to society.

Oprah is the chairman of:
Harpo, Inc.
Harpo Productions, Inc.
Harpo Studios, Inc.
Harpo Films, Inc.
Harpo Print, LLC
Harpo Video, Inc.

Oprah's Book Club—She has tempted people to read again. Her book club has encouraged people to read books they previously would never consider. Reading together with Oprah offers a connection and has opened up a new world of discovery.

The Oprah Magazine—Her successful magazine covers every subject imaginable to educate, uplift and inspire— encouraging readers to improve the quality of their lives.

Oprah's Angel Network—Orphanage Parties—"A Christmas wonderland for AIDS orphans. A celebration to let them know they are not forgotten—21 days...50,000 children...a million moments of happiness.... What Oprah calls 'the single greatest moment of my life.'" She encourages everyone to use his or her live to make a difference with her Angel Network.

The Oprah Boutique—All purchases benefit the Angel Network-order online. Click on The Oprah Boutique. Oprah has featured over 100 Charities on her show.

An O Group—On Oprah's home page, go to the left and click on O Group. And take a tour. The Groups are public or private place where you can connect with others. You create O Groups. You start the topics of discussion. Your group leads the discussion. Join an existing group or create one of your own!

FOR MORE DISCOVERY ON THE INCREDIBLE LIFE OF OPRAH WINFREY, TAKE A TRIP—HER WEBSITE:
Oprah's Website: www.oprah.com
Click on: About Oprah
Go to: Oprah's Bio

OPRAH WINFREY BIOGRAPHY
"Oprah Winfrey has already left an indelible mark on the face of television. From her humble beginnings in rural Mississippi, Oprah's legacy has established her as one of the most important figures in popular culture." The awards she has received are incredib*e*.

In addition—SCROLL DOWN AND PERUSE EACH OF THESE SECTIONS AND READ THE DETAILED INFORMA-TION ABOUT EACH STATION OF HER LIFE:

TALK SHOW PIONEER

ACTRESS

PRODUCER/CREATOR

MAGAZINE FOUNDER AND EDITORIAL DIRECTOR

OXYGEN MEDIA

EDUCATOR

PHILANTHROPIST

OPRAH ALSO HAS HELD PERSONAL GROWTH SEM-INARS FOR WOMEN ACROSS THE NATION.

UNBELIEVABLE!! Absolutely UNBELIEVABLE!!

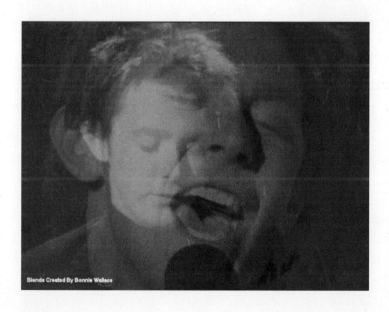

Blends Created By Bonnie Wallace

Gaye Deamer

Bonnie Wallace

CHAPTER EIGHTEEN

He's the perfect man— Perfect in that he's thoughtful, responsible, socially and politically conscious, educated, affectionate
and loving, sincere, has a huge heart, is giving and not to
mention incredibly handsome with a golden voice.

—Kimberly Locke

CLAY AIKEN—
YOU GET THE REAL DEAL

What is so endearing about Clay Aiken, as his life
unfolds—he's the "Real Deal." No pretense, nothing hidden,
nothing phony, rough edges and all. When one observes what
has happened to this child/man—mostly child at heart, it is
astounding. This former Raggedy Andy ventured into a maze
that has turned his life upside down. Many lust for celebrity.
Not Clay. The stage—and he has performed on many, was
enticing. But most fame is frangible, so he never embraced it.
Noticeably, he loved to perform and he contemplated attending

133

a Music Conservatory after high school but decided against it because he felt music didn't offer enough security. Clay found his niche in the world of special needs kids. He loved assisting their anonymous secrets out of obscurity—allowing a turn at normalcy. Kids also do not demand a forgery of personal change. When you live in the world of children, you can laugh and play and scramble and scrap and be a kid with the kids—that's the real Clay.

Conversely, fame embezzles your identity, your time, your psyche—you're always on display. Aiken's simple request is to go to McDonalds without a bodyguard—to merely walk through the golden arches and order his favorite hamburger. Clay said, "You always have to watch yourself, you don't even dare pick your nose because someone is always ready to take that picture."

Clay would love to live in Raleigh, his beloved North Carolina where he said, "people live at a slower pace," but that is not possible because he is mobbed at every stoplight. Everybody wants a piece of him and they are not coy in their demands. He has never lived in the fast lane, but he is now lives on that 75 mile-an-hour California speedway. He is co-renting a house in LA because people are so rushed he can sometimes slip through the gates without protection.

However, the tabloids slither around, just waiting for the famous to misstep. Most celebrities find it nearly impossible to stroll outside incognito because photogs stalk and hide in bushes, just waiting to take any picture they can exploit. This compulsion also from fans has been foreign to Clay Aiken because he admitted he never paid much attention to celebrities, plus he's never been very comfortable with crowds. When he was asked to name his favorite celebrity he stammered, then admitted the only person he could think of was Mr. Roger's of "In the Neighborhood Fame." He wished he could have his job. With all the phoniness that accompanies celebrity, we support and love what is genuine. He is that.

In one-breath Clay talks about his amazing experience and

Bonnie Wallace

in the next breath he confesses how miserable he sometime feels with all the attention. Aiken also remarked that his life is so over scheduled he oft times doesn't know what day it is. With good reason, Kelly Rippa (KR for Charisma) on *Live With Regis and Kelly* said to Clay, "People are wild for you! They are truly wild for you!" Tis' true. This wild acclaim however, can be a two-sided coin. It has to be intimidating for any normal kid who has never been star struck. How many newly crowned Super Stars would admit they cried for over an hour in their hotel room because they were so miserable with all the fanfare and because they no longer owned their life? Talk about an upside-down Cindereller story. However, once the clock struck twelve, Aiken is learning how to deal with the "ups and downs" of his famous ride. Even though his life is accessible for scrutiny, his behavior rarely makes a request for forgiveness—but it is seldom required. Newsweek called him, "refreshingly normal." Clay is not only refreshingly normal; he is refreshingly honest about the world that now engulfs him.

At any rate, his memoir continues to evolve. The reality— he lives in the diversity of Clay's world.... A few examples: In one segment of his life the news media films Clay Aiken as he gets out of a black limousine and makes the rounds with high-powered bigwigs at the nations capital. He stands stately before the political powers in Washington D.C. in a black designer suit, crisp white shirt and fashionable tie, standing as a states-man, giving an articulate presentation for Special Needs Kids. The dignified Aiken resembles a newly elected politician.... Then in another corner of Clay's world, this same 25-year-old kid, when he is privileged to go home, openly admits he loves to go to the North Carolina beach and play "hide-and-go-seek" with some of his old school chums.... Then in the next chain of Aiken events, Clay shakes the sand out of his "hide-and-seek" playwear and we view him on national television singing with such passion he creates irregular heartbeats in his adoring females and he is such a consummate entertainer, he causes women to rash.

Then there are added nuances in Clay's world.... He said he is not concerned what other people think of him. He contin-ued, "...as long as you're living right, then you don't have to worry about what people see." He has been hailed as a great role model for kids and he wears the WWJD (What Would Jesus Do) bracelet because he said it is a reminder of how he wants to live his life. He also said the LA influence will be a lot different than living in Raleigh. Some supporters are concerned with the LA influence.... Some fans were disappointed with the "bumping and grinding" that has taken place on stage and very upset about a jester of a picture that circled the Internet. Many fans were crushed. One mother said, "Clay presented himself as a role model, that's why we have supported him with our time and our hard-earned money. She continued, "A lot of Clay's support comes from families. We are so desperate for decent role models for our children. Let's pray he doesn't become another guttered, dime-a-dozen Pop Star." However, most fans believe in him and trust he won't repot the clay of who he is." Daniel Feinman of *Zap2it* TV News reported that Aiken had numerous TV offers to act, but he chose a cameo spot on *"Ed,"* because the show had the qualities he was looking for. Clay said, "I talked to a lot of people back home who were familiar with the show and the thing that resonated with every single person spoke to was how family oriented it was—something that everybody could sit down and watch it together." However, in the present "Sodom and Gomorra" world that surrounds us, Clay's admitted abstinence from promiscuity has resulted in some battering. When will you again hear a 25-year-old "Super Star" announce he does not condone premarital sex and it is more special if you save yourself for marriage? Another courageous note is that women throw their personals on stage and his cohorts tell him he could have a different girl in his hotel room every night and Clay says he would never take advantage of girls in that manner because he has too much respect for women. He also doesn't curse. Feinman said that Clay still has the veneer of "the boy next door," and he minds his language of even referring to "damn" as "The D-Word."

Diane Sawyer asked Clay if he had any faults. He thought for a minute then said he has a temper because he reprimands people when they curse, then added he has a habit of correcting people's English.... As a result, Religious leaders, parents and kids have waved their flags of support by buying so many CD's and tickets to his concerts his popularity has broken records.

Because Clay is a kid at heart—he sometimes acts kiddush and because he is not promiscuous, Aiken deals with "gay" bashing. On the gay issue, he clarified, "Because I don't give them any information, they have to make it up on their own—and they need something to talk about." He also said, "You are either a womanizer or you are gay and I am neither." Clay continued on Primetime, "Its high time there's somebody who represents people who aren't gay but who don't sleep around with everybody." Because he's clean, he doesn't smoke, he doesn't drink, he doesn't do drugs, he's not a womanizer, he is a target. He continued, "If I am supposed to carry the banner for all the nerds in world, I'm fine with that too."

In regard to Clay Aiken, this author's exhaustive research verifies HE IS NOT GAY. The accusations fly but there is not one thread of evidence to support the accusers—he's just a rare piece of Clay. He has never indicated a preference for men—he loves women. Amanda Drake has known Clay Aiken for years. It was reported she became furious and challenged a radio station that was doing some Clay/gay bashing. She cantered she has never seen any indications that he is gay. He has always shown great respect for women. Aiken said he hasn't dated much because he has always been shy in social situations and admitted he wasn't the type girls were chasing. When Clay appeared on the "The View" with the versatile host Meredith Vieira, screams erupted in the audience when he said, "I've always been kind-of-a nerdy guy." Then Clay added more frenzy when he said before *American Idol*, no girls were ever screaming for him.

Clay Aiken could presently date most girls on the planet, but he is on such a 94.1 FM's, Jagger and Kristi, said because breakneck schedule, he often suffers from sleep deprivation. Radio talk show hosts, Clay is in such demand he was harder to get on their show than "Sting." Clay laughed and during the interview he reiterated he wants his behavior and choices to emulate what his own children could be proud of. He wants to be an example for his own progeny. However, he will forever have the expected battles worn with celebrity and with the out-and-out-lies concocted by the tabloids—that comes with the territory. In some vicinities of his life he will always be vulnerable. However, Clay Aiken is Not Gay.

However vulnerable Aiken is forthright especially with his performances. On the night of the *American Idol* finals, when he performed the show stopping, "Bridge Over Troubled Waters," he hit the last stellar note—that almost brought the house down. When he was asked how that felt he said, "It hurt!" Some critics said his signature song, "This Is The Night," was cheesy. Clay said, he didn't care if it was cheesy, he never gets tired of singing the song because it recounts the amazing new life that has been handed to him. His album "Measure Of A Man," has applause but it also harnessed the usual critics who said the songs on the CD are sugar coated. Aiken ignores the critics and keeps the sugar on top of the charts. However, Clay's astounding success cannot be ignored, *Hits Daily Double* writes, "Indeed, Clay Aiken's RCA debut, 'Measure of a Man' is just plain huge-a whopper, a honker, a giant, beefy burrito of love." Possibly the critics should be the buyers who have paid for the album, because most buyers can't get enough of this man and his music.

Even though fame and fortune have been thrust upon him, Clay Aiken was never a big spender. The former college student

Bonnie Wallace

used to count pocket change to buy milk. However, he is now doing a little splurging. When you're invited to fly across the country in the Soign Corp jet and you're paid a reported 60-100k for a short gig—to open your mouth, sing a song and smile. And your single outsells most artists on planet earth except Elton John's tribute to Princess Diana. And your album "Measure Of A Man," goes Double Platinum the first week, with Clive Davis presenting you with the Double Platinum plague on *Good Morning America*. "You can buy what you darn well please."

The Clay bought a new silver Volvo convertible, an admitted mistake. He loves to ride with the top down, but going topless puts him in full view for the paparazzo's "Click! Click! Clicks!." Aiken was forced to close the lid on the California overhead breeze from the cameras, riding sidesaddle. He also tried to convertibly-California-parallel-park where the elfin spaces resemble mini homes for sparrows. (In Raleigh Clay said, "They don't parallel park; they just park.") Well the long and short of this park is—while Mr. Aiken was trying to squeeze his convertible out of the parallel dilemma, the paparazzi were having a hey-day flashing his every frustration. His fans have probably seen the episode in the Tabloids or on *America's Funniest Videos*. (Imagine having all of your foibles video taped and shown to the world—that's the downside of the 60-100k gigs?) To hide his head, shoulders, knees and toes from full view he then bought a white Volvo SUV. (Let's bet Volvo sales have picked up—lucky Volvo.) He also said he is a shoe whorse—possibly cars are going to come close.

Perhaps if Mr. Aiken occasionally exits his castle gate with a new make and a new color of car the paparazzi will not recognize him. Fat chance. They know that face and they will follow. Conversely, the producers gave him a $15,000 garish watch that he is embarrassed to wear. He said he would rather sell it and give the money to charity, but it was a gift so he says he had better not sell it.

This openness is what makes Aiken's adoring Claymates

fan the flames for his genial appeal. He says his greatest follow-
ers are middle age women who want to take care of him. It
tain't so—well sort-of-so—however, he must also include the
pubescent who want to stalk and cuddle his every move. And
then the seniors—they have found a fame they can trust and
someone who can flirt with their feelings again. Did we
mention a catch 22? Clay's Catch 22—his rabid fans have cat-
apulted him into super stardom. Without them he is a likeable
kid in Raleigh, North Carolina juggling to make ends meet.
With them his wealth and fame is staggering but he has to side
step many of the things he loves and he has to hover in many
unwanted places for refuge. His Catch 23—he genuinely loves
his fans and he gives them his plethora in appreciation.
However, he oft times does not know what to do with them,
there are so many—millions and multiplying. His Catch 24—it
is almost impossible to carve out some free time to exhale and
to spend some quality time with his family and a few trusted
friends.

Despite the catch phrases, Clay Aiken has caught on quickly
to the secrets of his appeal and he gives his fans what they
require for their partnership of affection. Their requirements:
Just sing-smile; whisper "thank you;" give oodles of shirt tugs;
do some knee bends with a few leg kicks; Growlllll now and
then in song; tremble—laced with a few lip quivers; dance with
the microphone; occasionally don a Fedora; make innocent love
to the TV screen with them as partakers; sign autographs; keep
the high moral standards (that's a biggie) and keep singing and
I promise you the Claymates will take care of the rest.... Most
men would love Clay Aiken's dilemmas.

And there are some....Dave and Geri of 95.7 WLHT Grand
Rapids radio, talked to Clay about diverting his life from his
love of teaching. Aiken said he saw some friends who were in
his University teacher-training classes. He admitted he felt
jealous knowing they will be in the classroom teaching—something he had anticipated doing for four years. (Imagine how
many of those college comrades would give their eyeteeth to

trade places with The Clay.) Greener grass, anyone? Geri also confirmed she tried to vote for Clay all night and could not get through. (There's very few who could get through, but of course that is well-worn news.) The same 95.7 Geri summoned Aiken back at the end of the interview and said, "Clay, pardon me, it's the mother in me, but don't disappoint us, you are such a role model for kids. You are so fabulous. Really! Don't disappoint us." Clay responded, "No pressure here. But I'll try my best."

The "real deal" who Clay Aiken openly displays is obviously what drove the stoic Simon Cowell bonkers. Clay's crowning resume when he entered the *American Idol* competition was he could sing, he was a momma's boy and he was high on special needs kids.... His future was safe because he had found his niche—the demand for good teachers is insatiable. No instability there.... On the other hand, Ruben Studdard was entertainment cool, he could have possibly been another "refrigerator" football star— he gave up a football scholarship to pursue his dream of becoming a professional singer. Plus, Ruben's signature was 205. He had his own group, "A Few Cats," and he was Pop Culture savvy—he had studied the industry. He had given himself five years to make it as a performer, therefore Studdard knew the ropes. (These are the suspicions why Ruben Studdard was Corporate elected to wear the *American Idol* crown—they didn't want to take a chance on a pop-naive, North Carolina schoolboy.) Another story was the gay issue—hardly, gays are not a real concern in today's voyeuristic world of entertainment—they should have saved their concerns because he is not gay.

Regardless, Ruben and Clay were great teammates because the only entertaining ropes CA knew was how to tie a square knot he learned at the YMCA summer camps.... Ruben had to tell Aiken what a big deal it was to be on the cover of *Rolling Stone*. Clay really didn't understand the significance of being showcased on every Pop magazine in the country. He said, "I don't get it, it's just my picture?" Gaining celebrity status wasn't on Aiken's list of meaningful goals in his life. Therefore, Clay Aiken did not understand what it meant to be tagged by *Top 40* James MacQuire, "the highly talented rag-doll/glamour puss."

But this kind of Clay is setting a different precedence in the music industry. Regardless, Aiken openly admits he is not the smooth type. If he were, he would merely clone all the other smoothies on the boardwalk. Allison Glock wrote in *Elle* magazine that some entertainers give Clay the willies because they are so smooth. The obvious reason— many observers feel they have to peel off three or four layers to get to some authentic skin. CA has no counterfeit layers—he is who he is. This genuine package of Clay Aiken was wrapped in his own unique naivety; it is also the ideal collection for the Claytrain who assertively patter to every step he takes. Clay admitted with Jagger and Kristi that he is not Pop Culture Savvy. They indicated that is what is so refreshing about him.

Funny, but Clay Aiken is savvy. It's obvious— he can distill to pulp every note he sings. When he performs, he knows how to tousle your heart, and the passion he exudes often catches you without breath. You exhale and melt when you thought you were past thawing.... He said he's never been in love. In the January 2004 issue of *J14* magazine, he was asked, "What is love to you?" He replied his cousin told him, "You'll know you're in love when you care about the person you are with more than anything else, more than yourself... and when you can't find the right words to say how you're feeling or you just can't understand why." Clay added, "I think that is what love is—when it's unimaginable to be away from the person, and you care about what makes them happy more that what makes you happy." He also confirmed, he's never had his heart broken. His fans swear his heart has been broken in a million pieces from the heartbreak he tenures in every song because Clay Aiken is a master of emotional recital.

Other mentions that are Clay Aiken savvy —he discounts the treasures of the world that hold many people hostage.

Gaudy possessions do not interest him. Neither do hip hop clothes because the continuing stripes and mismatched clothes stigma still lingers because mulderaiken's description of the fugly multi-colored jacket he wore on the "Independent Tour," created a lot of chatter in Internet chat rooms. However, when you co-headline a 30-city tour, nine-months after losing the crown on *American Idol* and your fans fill 80 to 90% of the nosebleed arenas with an average take of over $412,000 per show—who cares if your colors and stripes don't always match—most assuredly, not his fans. He has qualified he sometimes lets other people dress him. As a result, as the occasion warrants, he wears more style savoir-faire and he looks dashing in his designer duds. However, he is living, working and performing with the affluent. It will be interesting to see how he handles his wealth, fame, and his integrity of maintaining family values. His audience has great faith in The Clay. His first-rate common sense is much older than his now 25 years.

Regardless, there is Clay No.1 and there's Clay No. 2. We all have two sides. Those who have more than two sides, a No. 1—No.2—No.3—No.4 or more personalities, need to see Oprah's, Dr...you know who?

Clay No.1—He is a true gentleman and he is also all of the above. Week after week Simon Cowell belittled him in front of millions of people—he just stood there, said nothing—and absorbed the abuse. Then, he displays great respect toward everyone, especially women. He is this crisp clean-cut kid who looks and smells crisp and clean. Those who are privileged to breeze close to him, always remark how good he smells like whispers of Space NK....Clay was raised by a mother, father and grandmother who taught him true southern values coupled with true gospel principles. Plus, you cannot find a more devoted North Carolina mama's boy and he is a North Carolina mama's boy without an utterance of apology. No wonder. His mother said to him and it was printed in The Cary News, "You don't need to worry, Mom will worry for you."

The Clay also reprimands anyone who makes inappropriate

remarks, especially around children. On a radio talk show the DJ repeated some racy remarks his fans had made describing their CA obsession. Clay said, "Be careful what you say, there are children present." When any inappropriate conversations emerge, he corrects the interviewees immediately. His aplomb defends decency in full voice of his detractors. He has established and/or supports charitable foundations, namely; the Bubel/Aiken foundation for Autistic children and other organizations that support kids with special needs.

Clay No.1 admitted having a crush on *American Idol* contestant Carmen Rasmussen but indicated she was too young. But he told her to hurry and grow up so they could get married. Carmen, keep up your studies at BYU but stay in touch with CA....However, Aiken also expressed his affection for Kimberly Locke. In the "acknowledgments for his smash CD, "Measure Of A Man" he wrote to his friend Kim, "I Love you." However, he admits he has never been in love, and he confessed to Diane Sawyer, "I'm not confident enough to go after somebody and have her reject me." When he said that, you could hear the "THUDS!!" from around the planet. The Claymates were in a puddle. "Reject him, are you kidding?"

Clay No. 2—Don't be deceived by this fresh-face kid. Underneath that face is a very sharp young man. Again, he corrected the on-going brutal attacks from the vindictive Simon Cowell, with dignity. Most would have crumbled under the pressure. He marinated the criticisms and just kept getting better—through practice and from doing his homework. (To capture the heart wrenching emotions for his performance of "Solitaire," he called the song's creator Neil Sedaka, to ask if the man in the lyrics had committed suicide over the devastating loss of "his love".) The phone call resulted in Clay's stunning rendition of Solitaire becoming a best selling single. Trust Clay Aiken, he is still doing his homework; and he's creating his own personal montage regarding his astounding career.

Aiken is a charmer. But traveling with that fortuitous charm, his southern drawl doesn't miss a beat. And he is enormously competitive. Diane Sawyer asked if there wasn't a little biddy part of him that wants to outperform Ruben's album. He clearly hesitated then said, "probably a little," but he reiterated they would never let the album sales come between their friendship. He's also sure Ruben would like to outsell his album. Gary Graff, of "The Daily Oakland Press," interviewed Clay, and CA gave his usual gracious answer about his buddy. He said, "Yeah, I sold more singles than Ruben did, but his single got more airplay than mine...and we're not even competing in the marketplace 'cause we have two completely different markets." Ruben also gives credit to his pal when he said, "Clay's a great singer; man he can really sell you a song."

Aiken's competitiveness is also centered with his own performances. (But don't kid yourself his green eyes are wide open looking at all the competition and it surrounds him.) Clay admitted on *The View* he was checking the male contestants competing for *American Idol* 2004 for any serious contenders. He was concerned about having new competition. Coincidentally, the 2004 *American Idol* winner Fantasia Barrino was also from Clay's home state of North Carolina and Clay hosted the live party at the NC Greensboro Coliseum the night Fantasia won the AI crown.

At this point in his career Clay Aiken has been through his share of copious boot camps, regarding pop culture and the entertainment industry. The crash course is teaching him the ropes. When he signed a recording contract with RCA, he immediately hired a top entertainment attorney. He also added that Clive Davis the Music Maestro has taught him a lot. And let's not pretend naivety, CA keeps track of what his fans want from him and he is consciously satisfying those requirements for their unrelenting discipleship.

With good reason—Aiken told Gary Graff, "I don't want to be the '*American Idol*' Runner-up for the rest of my life, but I don't necessarily feel like I have something to prove." Clay has an amazing healthy self-image for someone who has experienced a history of rejection and indifference—not only from his biological father but also from girls and young peers. Faye Parker has to be given a mountain of credit because her son has tremendous self-confidence and he is not afraid to stand up to anybody including the powers who spearhead his future. And he is very smart at picking his battles. The bottom line—Clay Aiken trusts Clay Aiken.

Aiken is extremely disciplined, notably with his personal life and now with his career. After witnessing the professional mistakes of others including the instant release, then the embarrassing failure of the Kelly Clarkston and Justin Guarini movie, "From Justin To Kelly," he is methodically testing the waters for each new career move. Since his contract with *19 Entertainment* was not as binding because he didn't win the *American Idol* title, he later had more license to choose his representation, so in the spring of 2004 Clay added *The Firm* to his management team, a prestigious talent management company who merged in March of 2004 with the high-profiled, *Integrated Entertainment Partners.* Together, they represent an A-list of stars including Cameron Diaz, Leonardo DiCaprio and Robert Deniro.

American Idol judge Randy Jackson gave an interview with Elvis, on *Z Morning Zoo* and said, "Clay Aiken is the smartest one of them all," (indicating *American Idol* contestants). Jackson continued, "He is a very astute young man— very smart. He looks at everything, studies everything and pays attention to detail." Jackson said Clay has a shot of having a long career. However, Clay made it clear that he'll give celebrity his best shot and if it doesn't work, he'll go back to teaching, so he made certain in December of 2003 that he was awarded his diploma. A degree he had earned. Clay told Diane Sawyer, "I'm a realist not an optimist. I don't want false hopes." So he tries to stay on solid ground. Clay always underplays his fame because he realizes it can be fleeting.

His fans shouted, "Excuse us! Clay Aiken go back to teaching—become a school teacher?" The Clay Fans will not let that happen—they are totally crazy for OMC—(Our Man Clay.)

Just imagine when he is paid 60k and up, up and away it goes, to (sing a song and smile) then as a school teacher he'd have to teach for nearly two years to make about that same 60k—hmmmm. Sing, Clay Sing. Clearly, The Clay has passed the point of no return, for school teaching, anyway. Yes, his devoted fans have other plans for Mr. Aiken....

Regardless of his fame, there are other obvious glitches. The discontent of Aiken's celebrity is he often does not know what he'll be doing each day (each hour) or the next week. His management team programs his day-to-day schedules. This is difficult for a guy who likes to close the door for some privacy and a little solitude. But that lack of solitude has some rock-solid reality.... Clay Aiken would be back peddling if he didn't admit that his record breaking Cd sales, his sold-out concerts and his international fan base proves he was the AI victor. He is still introduced as the 2nd Runner-up, (which has to be a little unnerving at times because who's kidding who)? It is no longer a contest. The results are in loud and clear. He won, big, bigger biggest—yes, big time.

On the other piece of solid ground, *American Idol* gave us Clay No.1 and Clay No 2—his fans echoed, "We'll take both." Tom Ennis said 19 Entertainment's Simon Fuller's goal is to discover new talent to manage and nurture. Clay said of all the people who managed his career, he trusted Simon Fuller the most. And let's face it; Fuller's franchise has given us some refreshing new talent. It was reported that many Music Moguls despise *American Idol* because the AI winners are prefabricat-ed Pop Stars; therefore the singers have no credibility. No cred-ibility? Credibility in the music business obviously has little to do with talent. Music industry credibility seems to depend on how many years an artist has spent barhopping to make it to the top. AI winners, Clay Aiken, Ruben Studdard, Kelly Clarkston and Fantasia Barrino have spent most of their lives on stage, but according to celebrity standards they haven't groveled suffi-ciently. The industry seems to shout, if you haven't reeked of bar smoke and booze and have not been favored by nightly drunken applause year-in and year-out, you have not paid your dues. Some radio stations are also stuck in the same caves— some stations will not play much AI music.

What is so preposterous there are millions of Aiken fans who would stay tuned to the radio to hear him sing. Because he is seldom played on the stations, they turn off the radio and listen to his CD's. Regardless, radio DJ's also have their complaints. Mix 93.3 FM DJ, Kelly Urich pointed out the Clay fans are so militant in their support of their Idol they turn some DJ's off, so even if some stations like Clay, they won't play his music. They complain they get e-mails from all over the country. E-mails from fans from outside their listening area, asking them to play Aiken's songs. (The Claymates sent an alert into Cyberspace encouraging fans to call all their local radio stations and ask them to play his music because very few locations have him in their rotations.) Some stations are so bombarded with requests they get irritated.... This absurd dilemma is when the DJ's don't play Clay's music, the fans hound DJ's to play his music and because they hound them, the DJ's won't play his music. The situation is beyond ridiculous. Can't there be a compromise?

Many buyers are supporting gifted vocals without the filthy lyrics and satanic rituals. The demand for Clay's 2003 album release was so enormous that some stores limited individual CD "Measure Of A Man," purchases to no more than (3 per customer).

The shocking trend in the music business belongs to some Rappers and strippers who are willing to offer gutter-edge antics to keep their albums on the charts? Clay Aiken is the first artist to stand up and say, "I'm not going to compromise who I am for record sales." He has stood up to the highest powers in the music business and refuses to use filthy language and refuses to sing about sex and violence. He told *RCA Records*, "Don't go there with me." Time reports, "Aiken believes that since everyday people chose him as their hero, those at RCA, who don't like him or his music are biased against everyday people."

Clay continued, "I don't know why people relate to me, but my guess is that they're tired of beautiful, cookie-cutter pop stars." Richard Sander, executive vice president and general manager of RCA Records caught on early to Clay's emotional connection with the audience. RCA was going to sign Aiken regardless of the *American Idol* outcome, because he said, "I'm a disciple of the phenomenon."

Teenagers are a vast market, but every age of support for Clay Aiken proves they will fight for this decorum. Bravo for this courageous kid who has the fortitude to stand up to the music industry whose business was going in the toilet before *American Idol* brought on a medley of new talent who the public is willing to invest in. And Bravo for Simon Fuller, the Fox Network and Mr. Clive Davis.

"The Lord will fight for you; you need only to be still."
(NIV version)

Exodus 14:14

Bonnie Wallace

CHAPTER NINETEEN

It's important that I make a difference in some way.
If it's performing and touching someone that way,
that's great; if it's being a teacher and helping some
kid understand something, that's even better..."

Clay Aiken

HOW A COURAGEOUS YOUNG MAN IS
MAKING A DIFFERENCE

—THE BUBEL/AIKEN FOUNDATION
— ALL ABOUT AUTISM
AND A MYRIAD OF OTHER CAUSES
HE SUPPORTS

Clay Aiken created the Bubel/Aiken Foundation as an
avenue to reach out and help children with disabilities. He is
tireless in his efforts to help children and other organizations to
benefit those in need.

Here is a small sampling of his level of participation however, by the time this book is published based on his tract record, the list will probably have grown significantly:

In a special press conference on Capitol Hill: Clay spoke on behalf of Youth Service America for National Youth Serve Day. He presented an "Able to Serve" award to a young woman from Roanoke, Virginia who was disabled. Senator Harkin spoke in praise of Clay. He said: "While Clay's album may teach us the 'Measure of a Man' Clay's passion for service and community involvement teaches Americans how to be the 'Measure of a Nation.' The Under Secretary of Education Gene Hickok and the corporate CEO for National and Community Service were also present.

Stories for Heroes announced a partnership with Operation Christmas Spirit. "... the Arthur Celebrity Audiobook is... Stories Series for Heroes... read and recorded by celebrities such as Clay Aiken.... A majority of the proceeds... will benefit three children's charities: The Bubel/Aiken Foundation, National Education Association Health Information Network and the Elizabeth Glaser Pediatric AIDS Foundation."

Jeremy Borden wrote: "Aiken is helping the West Cabarrus YMCA launch a program ...(for) children with disabilities to participate in summer camp... (with) nondisabled kids.... The foundation launched "Project Gonzo" as a pilot program.... The YMCA helps... the cost of regular YMCA day camp... the Bubel/Aiken Foundation provides... extras to accommodate children with disabilities... (such as) a nurse and specially trained counselors....." As told by Susan Flanders, the YMCA's membership and marketing director.   Clay Aiken took a flight from London to participate in additional foundations. He was present at The Rosalyn Carter Institute for their magnificent inaugural Celebration of Caregivers Gala. Clay was an honored guest, but it was pointed out that the real heroes are all of those dedicated care givers who devote their time in taking care of others.

There are untold additional projects that Clay Aiken has or

will be participating in that are not mentioned but are very worthy causes. However, he is always personally involved in his Bubel/Aiken Foundation....

THE BUBEL/AIKEN FOUNDATION

OPENING DOORS—OPENING MINDS

THE MANY ARMS OF THIS GREAT FOUNDATION ARE OUTSTRETCHED TO ASSIST ALL CHILDREN WITH DISABILITIES WHO ARE IN NEED:

SEE THE BUBEL/AIKEN FOUNDATION'S OFFICIAL WEBSITE:

The Bubel/Aiken Foundation provides opportunities for individuals with autism and other physical and mental disabilities to participate in programs that are typically only available to those without disabilities. Through grants, youth programs, such as after-school and camping services, will be able to adequately train staff to work with individuals with special needs. The Foundation also strives create awareness about the diversity of individuals with disabilities and the possibilities inclusion can bring. Through collaborations with the disability, education, entertainment, and media communities the Foundation will recognize those whose commitment to breaking the stereotypes attendant to the developmentally disabled has broken barriers and extended the boundaries of the human experience for all.

The mission of The Bubel/Aiken Foundation is to provide services and financial assistance to facilitate fully the integration of children with disabilities into the life environment of those without. The Foundation will create awareness about the diversity of individuals with disabilities and the possibilities inclusion can bring. Through collaborations with the disability, education, entertainment, and media communities, the Foundation will recognize those whose commitment to breaking the stereotypes attendant to the developmentally disabled has broken barriers and extended the boundaries of the human experience for all.

Clay Aiken—Co-Founder
Diane Bubel-Co-Founder
Fran Skinner-Lewis-
The Foundation's Executive Director

LOOK WHAT LOVE HAS DONE (LWLHD) has contributed so much time and effort to this cause and is now part of the Bubel/Aiken Foundation.

How to contact the Foundation:

Mailing Address

The Bubel/Aiken Foundation
P.O Box 90307
Raleigh, North Carolina 27675
Phone: (224) 430-0950
Fax: (773) 777-9434

clay@bubelaikenfoundation.org

diane@bubelaikenfoundation.org

faye@bubelaikenfoundation.org

frances@bubelaikenfoundation.org

lwlhd@bubelaikenfoundation.org

customerservice@bubelaikenfoundation.org

tbafstore@bubelaikenfoundation.org

Send donations to:
Bubel-Aiken Foundation
PO Box 90307
Raleigh, NC 27675

Organizations that have received help or that continue to receive help: The Autism Society of North Carolina (ASNC) is another organization that is reaping the benefits from the Clay supporters. David Laxton, ASNC's Director of Communications and Jill Hinton Keel, Executive Director told of the generous donations that have been given to their Chapter as a result of Clay's celebrity. The organization has received generous donations plus revenues from auctions, illustrations, banners and from Clay Aiken memorabilia. Dorothy Brown, an employee at The Finley YMCA chapter said, "If I had to create the perfect YMCA spokesperson... I could not have created someone more perfect than Clay Aiken. He is so generous of spirit, so dedicated and so giving."
Many Generous Fans organize collective charities to assist those in needs Listed are the Foundations and Charities that will benefit from Operation Christmas Spirit staffed at ClaytonAiken.com (The ClayBoard), ClayAikenWorld.com and ClayDawgs:

WORLD USO (Services the children of the Armed Services)
Operation USO Care Package (services the troops overseas)
Toys for Tots
NEA-HIN
The Starlight Foundation
Judes Children Research Hospital
Operation Phone Home
The Library Donation Project

BECAUSE OF CLAY AIKEN AND HIS GENEROUS FANS
THE WORLD IS BECOMING A BETTER PLACE

CLAY'S DESIRE TO HELP CHILDREN WITH AUTISM IS
WHERE IT ALL BEGAN...

ALL ABOUT AUTISM

The Autism Society of North Carolina
505 Oberlin Road, Suite 230
Raleigh, NC 27605-1345
Tel: 919-743-0204, 1-800-442-2762
Fax: 919-743-0208
Website: www.autismsociety-nc.org
For the National Autism Society:
Website: www.autism-society.org.
See "Autism Society Chapters" for individual state and county
chapters.
The Autism Society of North Carolina is committed to provid-
ing support and promoting opportunities which enhance the
lives of individuals within the autism spectrum and their fami-
lies.
Autism and other autism spectrum disorders are developmental

disabilities that impair a person's ability to understand information and communicate with others. Autism spectrum disorders occur in as many as 1 of every 250 children born and is more common in boys than girls.

FROM THE AUTISM SOCIETY OF NORTH CAROLINA

What is Autism?
Autism is a developmental disability that affects a person's ability to properly understand what they see, hear, and otherwise sense. Autism primarily affects communication. People with autism typically have difficulty understanding verbal and nonverbal communication and learning appropriate ways of relating to people and, objects, and events.

Autism spectrum disorders are the third most common developmental disability following mental retardation and epilepsy. Autism spectrum disorders occur in 1 of every 250 people. It is four times more prevalent in males than females. Autism occurs in all races and socio economic classes. Family income, lifestyle, or education do not affect whether or not a child will be born with autism.

What are the Characteristics of Autism?
Characteristics may differ markedly from person to person, but will usually include the following:
Severe deviations in language development - Language is slow to develop and usually includes peculiar speech patterns or the use of words without attaching them to their normal meaning.
Severe deviations in understanding social relationships - Children with autism may not use eye contact in social interactions, may resist being picked up, and seem to "tune out" the world. This results in an inability to play with others and an impaired ability to make friends.
Inconsistent patterns of sensory responses - The child may appear to be deaf and fail to respond to words and sounds. At other times, a child may be extremely distressed by everyday

noises such as a vacuum cleaner or dog barking. The child may show insensitivity to pain and lack of responsiveness to cold or heat, or may overreact to any of these.

Uneven patterns of intellectual functioning - The majority of people with autism have varying degrees of mental retardation. Only 25% of people with autism have near-average, average, or above average intelligence. However, some may have peak skills - scattered things done quite well in relation to overall functioning - such as drawing, math, music, or memorization of facts.

Marked restriction of activity and interests - A person with autism may perform repetitive body movements, such as hand flicking, twisting, rocking, or spinning. This person may also display repetition by following the same schedule everyday, same route, same order of dressing, etc. If changes occur in these routines, the child may become upset.

What Causes Autism?
Autism is a brain disorder, present from birth. What causes autism in specific cases is still unknown. It is known that autism IS NOT caused by the psychological environment a child grows up in. Some research suggests a physical problem affecting parts of the brain that process language and information coming in from the senses. Other research points to an imbalance of some brain chemicals. Genetic factors are often involved. Some people have suggested that there are environmental factors at work and research is being conducted in that area also. Autism may be a result of a combination of several "causes."

Does Autism Occur in Conjunction with Other Disabilities?
Autism can occur by itself or with other developmental disabilities such as mental retardation and epilepsy. Autism is a disability on a continuum from mild to severe. The severity of autism, other disabilities and mental retardation will all affect a person's overall level of functioning.

Can People with Autism be Helped?
Yes. Autism is treatable. Early diagnosis and intervention is

very important. Studies have shown that all people with autism can improve with proper individualized instruction. There are a variety of treatment methods available that may help improve the person with autism's ability to understand information and interact with others. Most people with autism become more responsive to others as they learn to understand the world around them.

Can People With Autism Become Independent?
People with autism can learn many things through specialized instruction. Utilizing structured programs that emphasize individual instruction, many people with autism have learned to function at home and in the community. Some people with autism are able to have jobs, use public transportation, drive a vehicle and lead nearly normal lives

If you would like additional information about autism, visit the websites and go to the Resource Center and Links pages. You can also participate in training seminars and workshops. View the Calendar of Events to see what's happening in NC. The ASNC Bookstore also stocks over 300 titles on a variety of autism topics. You are encouraged to browse the book list and choose from our many informative titles.

Bonnie Wallace

Blends Created By Bonnie Wallace

CHAPTER TWENTY

Clay's Leather Charm Necklace From Paula Abdul:
The Charms:
Knowing who you are, what you want to say and not giving a
damn.
Sing your heart out as if no one's listening.
Dance like a fool as if no one's watching.
Good luck with your wishbone--you'll still need a backbone.
Be who you are--be that completely.
Find your inner peace.

FACTS & MORE FACTS

ABOUT CLAY HOLMES AIKEN

Name: Clayton Holmes Aiken/ Clay Aiken (formerly Clayton
Grissom).
Birthday: November 30, 1978. (He has the same birthday as
Dick Clark and Winston Churchill.)

Star-O-Scope: Sagittarius—Sagittarius is a crusader and wants to "Reform Society," shouting its beliefs from the rooftops. Sagittarius is the spiritual leader of the Zodiac being "high minded," and is very social, energetic, of higher consciousness and may be an agent, preacher, teacher or crusader.

Age: 25 (2003)

Hometown: Raleigh, North Carolina

Height: 6'1"

Weight: 145 lbs. plus

Hair Color: Red, after makeover, Brown.

Eye Color: Green

Mother: Faye Parker

Real Father: Ray Parker. (He died of pulmonary fibrosis July 4, 2002

Biological Father: Vernon Grissom (He died February 27, 2003 at age 68 of heart failure.)

Siblings: (2004) A younger half brother Brett 18, an older step sister Amy 32 and an older step brother Jeff 37.

Favorite Color: green

Fans Favorite Color For Clay: red

Shoe Size: 12-13

He is right handed.

Church: Leesville Baptist Church

Religious Conviction: His wrist embraces his grounded beliefs—he often wears a bracelet with the letters inscribed WWJD "What Would Jesus Do?"

Favorite Bible Verse: Exodus 14:14 "The Lord will fight for you; you need only to be still." (NIV version)

High School: Leesville Road High School, Graduating Class of 1997.

Education: Graduated (Dec. 2003) in Special Education from UNCC—University of North Carolina in Charlotte.

First Job: Bagging groceries at Winn-Dixie.

Additional Job: "CAP MR/DD worker" (The Community Alternatives Program for Persons with Mental Retardation/Developmental Disabilities, North Carolina).

Career Goals: Before *American Idol*: Teach kids for 6 years with special needs. Get a Master's Degree at William and Mary in administration and become a principal.

Personal Idol: His mother

What he misses most about home: His mother, brother, relatives, friends and Eastern North Carolina Bar BQ.

Teachers Who Had The Greatest Influence On Him: Miss Probst and Miss Stone had such a passion for teaching; there passion influenced his aspiration to be a teacher.

Goals: He is not an optimist; he's a realist so he never sets out-

Bonnie Wallace

of-reach goals for himself. He always under expects everything so he's not disappointed. However, he always wanted to be in the Macy's Thanksgiving Parade and he's done that. He wanted to have a second album. (No problemo.)

What Bothers Him: When people use incorrect English such as double plurals and double negatives.

If Clay Couldn't Sing, What Talent Would He Like To Have: "I wish I could draw like my friend Meredith, even her handwriting is art."

What Is Clay's Definition Of An *American Idol*? "Someone with a talent who leaves a mark on American society and inspires people to think, feel, love, act."

Greatest Lesson From AI Experience: Perseverance

Idol Mansion: "I am kind-of-the-one in here who's the goody-goody."

Foundations And Causes He Founded And/Or Supports: The Bubel/Aiken Foundation and other causes for kids with special needs. A Revolution for decency.

Career Idol: Mr. Rogers of "In The Neighborhood," fame.

Last Book He Read: "The Color Of Water" by James McBride.

Three People He Would Like To Have For Dinner: Jesus Christ, Mr. Rogers and Jimmy Carter.

Favorite Movie: "The Rising Place."

Favorite TV Show: *West Wing*

Favorite TV Guilty Pleasure: *Reba*

Pets: He has a border terrier named Raleigh. He used to have a goat named Zoe. She's resting in peace.

Cars: Silver Volvo convertible. White Volvo SUV.

Favorite Male Pop Artists: Elton John, Jon Secada or Peter Cetera.

Favorite Female Pop Artists: Crossover artists Shania Twain and Faith Hill. He would like to do a duet with Martina McBride.

Favorite Childhood Songs: "Mammas Don't Let Your Babies Grow up To Be Cowboys," sung by (Willie Nelson) and "Islands In The Stream," sung by (Kenny Rogers and Dolly Pardon).

Favorite Song: "When You Love Somebody."

Favorite Album: "Hourglass," by James Taylor.

Singing Style: A combination of Harry Connick Jr., Elton John, and Jon Secada.

A Skill He Would Like To Develop: Play the guitar.

Favorite Reading And Sitting Room: The John.

Political Views: Liberal

Favorite Foods: Spaghetti, macaroni and cheese, Krispy Kreme doughnuts, Cinnamon Toast Crunch, Fuji apples with peanut butter, yellow mustard.

Food he dislikes: Sushi

Favorite Fast Food Hamburger: McDonalds
How He Likes His Steak Cooked: Medium well. His doesn't like his steak mooing back at him.
Favorite Gum: Dentyne Fire Spicy Cinnamon
Favorite Bedtime Snack: Ice Cream and milk.
Ice Cream Named In Clay's Honor: "Clay's Croonin' Carolina Crunch"
Favorite Pizza: Pepperoni
Favorite Drinks: Coke, Mountain Dew
Food Allergies: He's allergic to mint, chocolate, coffee, shell fish, mushrooms, almonds and other tree nuts.
Favorite Cologne: Space NK—a modern, rich, woody oriental aroma with a touch of cedar wood, patchouli, fir balsam and musk, refreshed with bergamot, lavender and cinnamon, and with a hint of nutmeg and clove—a warm, spicy, woody scent.
Hair Style: Spiked with a flat iron, Bedhead hair spray, and a touch of wax. (Plus Clay has a new secret Cologne. HMMMM.
Nickname: Gonzo
What He Misses About North Carolina: He misses family and friends and he misses the changing of the seasons. He loves spring, the snow and the changing of leaves in the fall.
Adjustments Of Living In LA: The horrible traffic. The seasons are the same. The hurried and crazy life of the people.
Favorite Video Game: Dead or Alive 3.
Most Unusual Skill: He can turn his feet around backwards.
Personal Assessment: He says he's plain and boring.
Phobias: cats, aqua phobic —afraid of large bodies of water.
Quirks: He used to bite his toenails until a pedicurist demonstrated there was a more appropriate method. A fan reported that Clay seems to be quite orally fixated. He grinds his teeth, bites the insides of his mouth, bites his lip, bites his nails, he constantly has his fingers around his mouth, nibbling on them.
Self Indulgence: He considers himself a shoe whorse—he owns lots of shoes.
Relationship Status: Single and loving it.
Worst Roommate: He had a roommate who reused his toilet

paper and he left it on the counter.

Feels About Life: His "to-do" list is still unfinished.

Free Time: Presently: sleep. Before AI: Art, Museums, Theater, Dine with friends, go to movies, listen to music, spend time with family, vegetate, sleep!

Dream Vacation: His Couch.

Fantasy Dressing Room: A quiet room with a sofa long enough for him to lie down on.

If There Were A Holiday In Your Honor (Clay Aiken Day. What Would It Celebrate? Volunteerism.

Clayton is the #253 most common male name.

Around 73,500 US men are named Clayton!

Clay is the #464 most common male name.
0.021% of men in the US are named Clay.
Around 25,725 US men are named Clay!

Aiken is the #2449 most common last name.
0.005% of last names in the US are Aiken.
Around 12,500 US last names are Aiken!
source: namestatistics.com

Bonnie Wallace

THE LIGHTER SIDE

CHAPTER TWENTY-ONE

Laughter is an instant vacation.

Milton Berle

THE PRESTIGOUS LADIES SUPPER CLUB

Ms. Flo belongs to a Ladies Supper Club that includes a dozen single friends. It is aptly named, "The Lucky Dozen." The Club has dined together for years and once a month the girls get-together to eat and shoot-the-bull. Flo said, "Don't get me wrong, we don't just eat once a month because we all have healthy shapes—it's just when we get together, an eating frenzy takes place that lasts for six solid hours. We discuss world affairs and other torrid affairs in the community and of course we eat and laugh ourselves into indigestion."

However, Flo pointed out that after a wonderful dinner and heartfelt night of purring about the joys of being single minded, some Spoilers ruined the entire evening. She reported that tension filled the room and a few people got hurt." She confirmed, "My vocal cords were strained, I had damaged shins—some lady kicked me into a limp and I was in pain." She bris-

(c) Michael Morgan

tled, "When you dine with a bunch of illiterate women who sit in their cubby-holes of life and have no clue of what's going on in the world—the world meaning the famous AI (*American Idol*) every Tuesday and Wednesday night, with the biggest Fox-jocks on Planet Earth from January to May-middle, it sets my menopause on fire."

Flo continued, "When I challenged their AI literacy, a good number turned on me. It is obvious that several of the Domed Diners live in lah lah land because the current world affairs just whistle over their be-wigged heads." Also, "Let me share why I am further disgusted."

"There are two Flo's in the house where I live. Not really a split personality—just a dual person who supports both sides of Flo's World." Continuing, "There's Flo No.1.... This Flo is kind, giving and loves her children and grandchildren; pets; especially Goose, Mark and Courtney's Muppet; Ruben's "A Few Cats;" and other things that are near and dear to her heart.... Then there's Flo No.2 who is always ready for Battle. No.2 always wears a protective shield and she'll pick up the sword at the drop of a hat, to defend Flo No.1, especially when Flo No 1 is being taken advantage of, is abused, (kicked under the table), called names, spat upon or suffers from any other injustices. Flo No. 2 has been up the trees of life and she is skilled in defending her better half. She admits that her better half is the other half of herself."

The gentle Flo No.1 was sitting with her friends, joining in the evening's small talk and savoring the last luscious bites of her "Dome of Chocolate" The dessert the Dome is famous for, when Flo No.1, smiled and made a simple but emphatic declaration of her obsession with Clay Aiken and commented that she was still irritated that he was robbed of the *American Idol* crown.

"Who's Clay Aiken?" One woman blurted with her eyes swirling up from her knit and pearl, who knits 24 hours a day, even when she's eating.

"WHO'S CLAY AIKEN!!!????" Flo No. 2 YELLED SO LOUDLY in this highfalutin restaurant, the fire alarm almost went off. People jumped up with fear in their eyes and shouted "What was that? A foot underneath the table kicked Flo's shin so forcefully she almost collapsed with pain. She flung upright and lost her last bite of the Dome as she spat chocolate sprays across the table and yelped with disbelief, "WHO'S CLAY AIKEN? HAVE YOU BEEN LIVING IN SIBERIA! WITH BOMBS GOING OFF IN YOUR HEAD!!??" Flo's varicose veins climbed to her neck. Her double chin flattened as her best

(c) Michael Morgan

friend grabbed her arm and jerked her down to a sitting position. Her friends across the table were wiping the sprayed chocolate out of their hair when a man at the next table raised his voice and arrogantly chortled at the top of his lungs *"I voted for Ruben!"*

"Well, that did it!" The restaurant was flabbergasted and watched for the attack as Flo picked up her big white linen napkin and marched toward big mouth's table, hell-bent on smacking him across his speckled baldhead. Suddenly, a woman emerged in a big bulky sweater and cut Flo in mid-attack and said, "Wait! I have something I want to show you. Flo stopped cold in her tracks and challenged, "Show Me What?" The stranger said quietly, "Follow me." She walked to the front of the dining room and announced loudly to the restaurant filled with patrons of elegance. "Look what I have!!"

Everyone gasped as the model flung open her big bulky floor length sweater with fear that she was going to expose herself. And she did! There in stunning Technicolor, painted all-up-and-down the front of her white iridescent T-shirt was a picture of The King of AI—you guessed it. There exposed, was a gorgeous gigantic facescape of Clay Aiken smiling back at Flo, that said, "Marry me!" She blurted, "I will, I will!" She wanted to kiss his soft cheeks but she was afraid she'd miss and be accused of you-know-what?

Flo had her female friend model Clay all through the restaurant, and then they both strolled over to Knit and Pearl where Flo held open the large sweater and said smiling, "I'd like to introduce you to Clay Aiken, the King of Pop." Knit and Pearl looked at the model and said, "Who on earth gave you a name like Clay?" Flo countered, "Take those knitting needles out of your hot pads and get a life."

Well, the long and short of the evening is Flo and her friend perused the restaurant and by the end of the perusement, everyone was introduced (in Technicolor) to the new King of Pop. But Flo admits her shins still hurt, and she's still Aiken, but she said, she'd, "Aik any day for Clay."

Michael Morgan
(c) Kick those legs GUY—AND shake your bootie!!

THE LIGHTER SIDE

CHAPTER TWENTY-TWO

Even if there is nothing to laugh about,
laugh on credit

Author Unknown

INSTRUCTIONS OF HOW TO VOTE
DURING THE 3-HOUR FINALE

Clacki (an admitted Clay addict) tells her story:

" I admit I am a true Clay aficionado, so I searched the web and found numerous websites that gave detailed instructions on how to vote the night of the AI finale. The information was written down, plus I added a little stratagem of my own.

"The night of the 3-hour voting marathon arrived....
"Tension was in the air! I hosed my hot flashes! Put my Menopause on hold. Tore open the box of Depends. (How do you put them on?) I gritted my teeth and got ready for the battle."

MICHAEL MORGAN

(c) Clay——nail clippers only cost 99cents

VOTING INSTRUCTIONS:

(1.) Tell family, friends and foes not to call Wednesday night during the voting vigil from 9 p.m. to 12 p.m. CST.

(2.) Don't drink anything after 9 p.m. No potty brakes are allowed. Drain your bladder before 8:50 p.m.

(3.) If your mouth gets dry from lack of sup, just think of Clay winning the AI crown and your mouth will salivate just envisioning his Coronation. If your mouth doesn't respond take a swig after midnight.

(4.) Tell your husband to get out his cell phone and vote or ...you guessed it!

(5.) Have several phones handy—and have all children who cannot be bribed—in bed. For those who are bribable and tall enough to reach the phone, offer an M&M for each redial. No M&M's during the 3-hour vigil. The reward comes when the clock strikes 12. This adds to the true Clay Aiken Cindereller Story.

(6.) Don't have food near your phone. You need both hands to vote—use the right hand to push the on/off speaker button and the left for the redial button. If your stomach starts growling say, "Down girl, food comes later."

(7.) If your fingers go numb from the 3 hours of redialing, dip them quickly in Tabasco sauce in between the button pushing mania, but DO NOT! Repeat! DO NOT touch your eyes. Red Eyes are for Midnight Flights only.

(8.) If you fall asleep from pure exhaustion make sure your head is directly above the phone so when your head snaps it hits the redial button. When you wake up from the jolt, DO NOT! DO NOT! allow the busy signals of lah lah land lull you back into a coma.

(9.) If you need a friendly voice to keep you awake, dial the competitor's number. That friendly voice that says, "Thanks for voting for Contestant No.1 will always answer and the shock that you've actually voted for Clay's competition will keep you awake for another 200 dials.

(10.) If you suspect hanging Chads after the voting has stopped, quickly clip them off your phone, or it could ruin this election.

A SIDE NOTE:

Clacki confessed, " I broke the rules because I had not eaten dinner before the voting started. Because of the excitement, I had lost my appetite plus, I started to hyperventilate (paper or plastic? I had plenty of the brown bags handy) just thinking about the 3-hour marathon. Health professionals counsel to feed your body every two hours to keep your Metabolism on fire. When I felt my flames turn to charcoal I turned to the children's bowl of M&M's because my children are gone. I'm an empty nester—there are no birds at my house. So I cheated, but yet I didn't, because I kept the bowl of M&M's right below my tongue. When the charcoal within me started to smolder, I never dared let my right hand leave the redial buttons, so when I would hear the duh, duh, duh, busy signal. What else is new— I quickly dropped my tongue down and graced the tip with one M&M. I was following the advice of my diet counselor. She said, 'Never, ever gobble-up large mouthfuls of food. Take little bites and chew like crazy. The aggressive chewing lets the stomach tell the brain (which ever comes first) it is satisfied.' Now, my desire was to follow my counselor's advice during these crucial 3-hours of no-potty breaks, no water and of total starvation.... My goal was to flick my head perfectly so when my head dropped, the head snap would perfectly tattoo a M&M on my tongue. As a result, I let each M&M dissolve in my mouth as slowly as possible to keep the embers burning. The embers stayed hot all night long but were doused the next day when it was announced that Clay had lost the crown to his competition.

Clacki confessed, "Finishing this 3 hour vigil, I learned a lot about devotion and a little of what the devoted Clay Fans have gone through to keep Clay on top."

THE LIGHTER SIDE

CHAPTER TWENTY—THREE

A laugh is a smile that bursts.

Mary H. Waldrip

A CLASS IN APPRECIATION

Barbara Streisand's popular rendition of, "People who need people are the luckiest people in the world," became heated debate among Psychologists. They argued, "People who need people are not the luckiest people in the world." Many beg to differ. Regardless of the debate, some people need people. Entertainers need people. And they need to show them their appreciation—if with only with a mere, "Thank You!"

Fans choose their objects for affection. Celebrities don't choose— the public decides! Fans endorse personal pledges of adoration, but they are also fickle. They are often looking for their next Idol. However, an injection of appreciation is often all that is required for most of their ceremonies of worship.

Some entertainers' strut, like their celebrity was merely

created by osmosis, or by some magical feat-oops! Let's reword that, because it's those magical feet who rush to buy their movie tickets, CD's, albums, T-shirts and bobble-heads or anything else they can capture to immortalize.

Michael Morgan

(c) The Trio of *American Idol* Judges—Randy, Paula and He smiles—the Simon Smiles

Celebrities often forget who is responsible for their stardom. Possibly, some reminders are necessary. Some Celebrity classes might fill the bill.

Keep in mind all the "Classes of Appreciation" don't have to be taken at once. The classes offered are:

Class one: "Thank You!"

Class Two: "I Appreciate You!"

Class Three: "Without You I Am Just Another Wannabe."

Class Four: "Without You I Am Just Another Has Been."

Brian Charlesworth

Simon-You're just not the type of Pop Star we're looking for.

Taking all four classes at once could be overwhelming so we offer Class No. 1.

Let the first class begin and don't be afraid to let the instructor assist you....

The "Thank You" Class.... (Take a deep breath.) Let's start the class with just the first word, so you don't feel overwhelmed....Thank is not that hard to pronounce. To start, just barely open your mouth and put your tongue under your two front teeth. Now concentrate—it's not that hard. Again, put your tongue under your two front teeth and gently blow and make a "thhhhhhh-hh" sound. Practice that several times. When you've got that down pat, don't pat anything, just keep the "thhhhhhhhh" sound going. Now add a vowel—not a loud bursty reverberation--don't frighten yourself because you've never practiced the "thhhhhhh" sound before, let alone a "thank you." Just add a low purring sound as you practice, because you don't want to initiate a startle. Now concentrate and add a Looong "aaaa" to the blowing, purring "thhhhhhhhh" sound. Now, Practice! Practice! Practice! When you have the "thhhhhhhhhhaaaaa" so it's familiar in your mouth, curve your

mouth down when you add the "n." Right on, now say "thhh-hhhhaaaannn." Again, "thhhhhhaaannn." Good, good, good....
Then for the finale of the Thank put a brisk "k" on the end.
Well, not too brisk or they might think you are coughing or
snorting, which ever comes first. But just remember to brisk it!

When the brisk-its are done. (Yum. The smell is mouth
watering.) Hush! Now keep going. Now put all the parts
together. The thhh— the long "a"— the "n"—and the brisssk it.
Now say them all together.... "ThhhhhaaaaaannnkkkKiskit!
Stop! Don't add the "Kiskit on the end. Just brisket the K.
Again, "ThhhhhaaaaannnK! Good! Wow! Great! You did it!
Say, it again Sam, with a little softer "k." Again,
"Thhhhhaaaaaannnkkk!" Wow! "I like you. I really really like
you!" And so will your fans.... See it was not that difficult!
Nothing is difficult if you just know how to do it. Now for the
next lesson!

This is the You class that goes on the end of the Thank with
a small space in between the Thank and the You. You know
what I mean. Just don't squish them together. This class is not
as difficult as the Thank class because it's all about You. People
are You-s, and of course Entertainers are You-s because it's well
known that some Entertainers really You-s people, especially
their fans, through lack of appreciation. Hopefully, this class
will be helpful.

Class comes to order! The You Class has now begun....
Open your mouth wide, don't say "ahhhhhh," just open sort-of
like Simon did when he sucked-up the face of the adorable
Paula Abdul for the *American Idol* 2003 finale. Wait! Wait!
Wait! Don't open your mouth that wide! If you're determined
not to duplicate the "Simon, swallow me up baby" mouth
approach to form the You on the end of the Thank, do the
Simon—then gradually bring Simon down into a medium-sized
pucker. Once your mouth is puckered properly—be sure to
breathe out and purr at the same time with a long sounding
"uuuuuuuu".... Don't be concerned about the spelling, everyone
knows how to spell You! It's just hard to teach people how to

spell it when the y and the o are silent? Now let's hear it for the U— (This U is not University born) it's the famous You that follows the Thank.   Okay, let's practice.... Open the Simon—-Get ready! Get Set! Go!!!! Okay, now bring him down slowly to a pucker. Now breathe out and purrrrr at the same time "uuu-uuuuuuu." Gotcha. Perfect—— Now the trick is putting the Thank and the You together.

Remember in the first class, the 'thhh"— the long "a"—the "n"—and the brisssk it. Now, remember how we put them all together. "Thhhhhaaaaaannnkkkk!"   Now say it! Say it again slowly——"Thhhhhaaaaaannnkkkk!"   Okay, okay, okay, hang on to it—not to lose it. Let's hurry and add the You.... Form the Simon—-Get ready! Set! Go!!!! Okay, take Paula's face out of his jowls and bring him down slowly to a pucker. Now breath out and purrrrr at the same time "uuuuu-uuuu." Gotcha. Perfect. "This Is The Moment." Now put them together. I will lead you. I wish I had some music—It's Somewhere Out There. This is no time to play around. Let's say it together, "Thhhhhaaaaaannnkkkk!" "uuuuuuuuuu!"   Good. Good. Good. Now let's do it with no Exclamation Point and lets keep repeating and shortening it slowly so we can get it right. Okay, "Thhhhhaaaaaannnkkkkk uuuuuuuuuu."   Again—'Thhhhaaaaannkkuuuuuu." Oooops! Remember the space.... Again. "Thhhaaaannkk uuuu." Better. Again—"Thhaannk uuu." The last time,loudly—"Thank You."   Wow, you did it!!

Thank You! Thank You!   Honestly, what fans simply require is a mere Thank You.

Gaye Deamer

Michael Morgan
(c) Clay's Favorite Reading Room

THE LIGHTER SIDE

CHAPTER TWENTY-FOUR

Humor is the harmony of the heart.

Douglas Jerrold

WHAT CLAY AIKEN HAS TAUGHT HIS FANS

Spice NK is not used to sprinkle on toast.

Stars and Stripes are no longer just for flags.

Polka dots are not to be worn outside.

Lip bite is not a mouth disease.

Don't lose your keys - they could end up in Fugi.

A cell cert is not a breath mint.

Dorks know how to pick up the fun.

Caressing Mic is for women drools only.

Performing in a concert with 10,000 screaming women is hard on the ears but good for the heart.

Cover up is no longer a term just for Enron.

Sleep deprived people can conk out - even on Capitol Hill.

Shell pink lips have nothing to with the Ocean.

Dog puppets that smoke cigars are out to lunch.

Platinum is no longer just a hair color.

If you are the only boy in your choir class, you can still have fun.

A Coliseum was made for 145 lb. Gladiators.

Being from NC doesn't make you the Andy Griffith show.

Tearing up can also make the man.

A Rolling Stone (cover) gathers no moss.

Winning E.W.'s "10 People To Watch," was corrected by fans as "There's only (1) person worth watching."

Glory never comes from falling, but from rising off the platform.

Ruben could you please teach Clay to eat more than one meal a day?

(c) Michael Morgan

Hockey is okay for ice skaters.

Green Eyes are more than a song title.

Wedgies do not inflict pain.

Bridge Over Troubled Water has been renamed to "Bride Over Liquid Gold."

Cats are just cats.

It was an accident PETA.

This Is The Night has been renamed "This Is Just The Beginning."

There is absolutely nothing wrong tripping over your own feet.

The sound of doves crying is actually the sound of women thudding en masse.

Moose is not only found in them thar hills.

Before ascending on top of a lift, make sure the power is on.

Hot Pockets are considered the ultimate in fine dining.

DMV line hopping is still allowed in Raleigh.

Perusing the Clay board is not boring.

Lost and found was never found.

A grunt is not grungy.

Never, and I mean never, let them see you burp.

Old driver's license photo—very very scary.

Playing the air guitar and the air drums is cool. Who knew?

Hong Kongers who have your new drivers license photo questioned, "Who's Dat?"

DJs can have split personalities.

Giving a child a life is more important than fame.

Long eyelashes on men are long eyelashes on only a chosen

few.

CA does not stand for California.

Britney Spears came on Kimmel with some clothes on.

Idol found. Game over.

Polka dots, flannels and Clay are a trio.

Bumping and Grinding is not always performed in a dentist's chair.

Temper tantrums can inflate many hearts.

Solitaire is the only game in town.

The Ruben Sandwich was really not named after Ruben.

Simon wears XX small T's to show off his workout results.

We're here to open doors and open minds.

The Firm is no longer just on The New York Times Bestseller list.

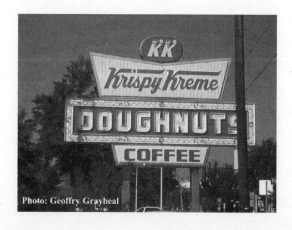

Photo: Geoffry Graybeal

Being invisible brings out the man.

Nothing can ever be so wrong that can't be fixed or ignored!

Freckled dryer sheets are hot sellers.

Not everyone will tell you his or her favorite color.

Living on a bus with me is not hard.

Michael Morgan
(c) GO CLAY! TUG - TUG, TUGS=SCREAMS! SCREAMS!
SCREAMS

There is someone out there who can out-talk The Clay.

Being a chatterbox sells tickets.

We're here to open doors and open wallets.

Unchained Melody has unchained a lot of hearts.

Eating only one meal a day is not a weight gainer.

Freckles are sexy.

Having a dozen videos on hand, does not hurt the hand.

Cinnamon toothpaste is as cool as mint.

 Nutritionists are correct—Grease can raise women's blood pressure.

Buttercup is not just a flower.

Triple undershirts hides the skin.

Wearing a Fedora does not hide the man.

Flip Flops are more than a blundered high dive.

Few schoolteachers, if any, get chased through malls.

Losing everything, including the AI title has proved very beneficial.

He is used to women taking care of him—who'da guessed?

Screaming for two hours straight is good for the fan lungs.

Wearing the same thing more than once in public is not taboo.

Boat oars are not just for paddling.

"Guest two's" are better than "Guest One's."

Is okay to run around with guards.

Baseball pitches do not have to go over the plate.

Paisley fabric is not just for curtains.

Michael Morgan

(c) Ruben not only has a velvet voice, he holds the name of the famous Ruben Sandwich

Talking to strangers on cell phones is dangerous.

Wearing glasses does not make a nerd.

Having a messy room is no longer attached to teenagers.

The song, "The People On The Bus," was not written just for Kindergarten Kids.

Eating junk food does not turn some people into junk.

Ears are for more than holding up glasses.

Mint is mind-boggling.

Weighing in at 145 lbs is just for the light-minded.

Skinny men can hold their own.

Stubble no longer means a short butch.

Wearing a bracelet has family-fan support.

White skin is now in.

Suntans don't make the man.

Seeing Sedaka cry, made everyone cry.

One person can put a Southern State on the map.

Winn-Dixie is not a cheer.

Getting a Master's Degree can result in a cut in pay.

It's okay to miss North Carolina Bar BQ.

Being a realist and not an optimist has its benefits.

Screaming for two hours straight is not good for naggers.

It's okay to under-expect things in life, not winning was an under-expected bonus.

There were no turkeys in the Macy's Thanksgiving Parade.

Every great song in America will have the C.A. stamp.

Skinny guys are bigger and better..

Saying ain't, still ain't good English.

It's okay to correct other people's English when they use double plurals and double negatives.

The John has become a favorite library stop.

It was okay to be a 'goody goody' in the *American Idol* mansion, voters noticed.

All your fans are welcome "In Your Neighborhood."

You said you liked *West Wing*, tell that to Kentucky Fried Chicken.

Yellow mustard is not just for Hot Dogs.

The order of "I'll take pizza, but please hold the mushrooms"- keeps a lot of hands in a holding pattern.

Red leather and hip shakes are a dangerous combination.

Waxing is no longer connected to a floor scrub.

It's okay to tell Simon you prefer him with his mouth closed.

The steak that moos back has caramel configurations.

Hoodies are a vital part of one's wardrobe

 Eating ice cream and milk for a bedtime snack does not turn a person vanilla.

A great singer knows how to Kyrie himself with the crowd.

Chicken wings do not satisfy a starving man.

Allergic reactions are like giving birth out of your chest—personal birthing is a remembered experience.

At *Star Bucks*, sipping a chocolate coffee with a touch of mint, sprinkled with chopped almonds can give a quadruplet reaction.

It was okay to tell Randy Jackson he's a mean dude.

Bed head is no longer hair sticking up after the alarm goes off.

It's not nice to watch other people in their room.

Horrible traffic has become very profitable.

If you don't succeed in Charlotte, try again in Atlanta and give it another shot in Hollywood.

Red heads are in.

The announcement of a new secret cologne can turn the Internet into a guessing-game frenzy.

Here's to not caring.

Noses can be exquisite and lips can be to die for.

Michael Morgan

(c) Here kittie, kittie, kittie—Nice kittie...

Turning your feet around backwards, takes the right foot forward.

Gonzo is suddenly sexy.

"Plain and boring," has been redefined in Webster's Dictionary.

How a 6 1" (73 inch) guy can be afraid of a (12 inch) cat.

Eating a few vegetables never hurt anybody.

Agua phobic is now re-defined as the new wave.

An image is not how you look, it's what you do and say.

Phone interviews look best if you're in your pajamas.

A large body of water is not in a glass.

Biting your toenails is not tasty.

Toe Nail clippers only cost 99 cents.

If you want to make God laugh, all you have to do is tell Him your plans.

Stealing cars makes dad mad.

Reused toilet paper is still a turn off.

Being a mic stand can be hazardous to your health.

That a "to do" list is never too done.

A dream vacation is a very expensive couch.

Exhaustive phone interviews have become famous.

Regardless of how bad the music sounds, there is a lesson to be learned.

Glory notes are now found in the thesaurus.

It's ok to want to be like Mr. Rogers. Just stay out of his neighborhood.

Krispy Kreme donuts are Not the best things to come out of North Carolina.

An *American Idol* is for skinny dudes.

Fans licking the mic post-show doesn't cause trench mouth.

It's okay to lose a Scrabble game.

You can drown in the bathtub even if you're over 6 foot.

McDonald's in Ireland has crappy hamburgers and sucky French fries.

You can never wear too many layers.

As long as you are living right, then you don't have to worry about what people see.

Fame might get you to the head of the line at the DMV, but it can't guarantee you a good picture.

A flat iron has made pressing clothes extinct.

The Fedora was not designed for flaps.

Clack is a secret weapon.

It's not a competition.

Watch out for old men with canes. They attack.

The bus and Jay Leno feels like home.

There is virtually no song that wouldn't sound better if Clay sang it.

Grocery stores do more than sell food—they sell pandemonium.

Air instruments create mega air screams.

Contacts do not hide those eyes.

2nd place can be a very good thing.

There is no such thing as too many stripes.

Big talent can come in skinny packages.

The big question. What's your favorite brand of milk?

Bonnie Wallace

Clay Aiken
The Heart Factor

White suits are heavenly.

"The Shadow," doesn't live here anymore.

Pink shoelaces look cute on men.

Strips, plaids and paisleys are now popular for male doll clothes.

Glasses do more than provide better vision.

Women love the stubble. They love stubble, they love trouble.

Dawgs are good. Cats are everywhere.

Can't dance means, "Who cares?"

Blank videos are a women's security blanket.

Treat all women with the utmost of respect. They'll beat your door down.

Getting front row tickets shouts, "Thou Shalt Not Covet...."

It is perfectly normal to wear pajama pants when going out in public (as long as you smell good).

Uncool has become very cool.

Teaching is the noblest profession, but not in the classroom for OMC.

The big dawg has entered the building.

Wearing a Cheesehead is not cheesy.

Can't dance? Let me be your partner.

Driving around Los Angeles in a convertible can raise others accidental insurance.

Big men show their muscles, true men show their heart.

Women love freckles (I wish I knew that growing up.)

 Mothers know when to pull out the wrong pictures at the right times.

To shop or not to shop even at 3 am, that is the question.

Paper or plastic? Who cares, where can I hide?

Tucking your foot under on a leather chair can hurt—leather.

That Aiken wink gets 'em every time.

Glasses make some people look smarter.

Wearing a hoodie doesn't get rid of the stares.

Bracelets are now the new conscience.

 Beware of journalists that are both jaded and have no face.

When someone tells you to follow your dream, say "It worked!"

When you become a celebrity, all you have to do is mention a product and you own the company.

 Mothers know how to keep Pop Stars humble.

The booby picture was a berry berry big blunder.

It is okay to "thud" as long as we can thud with you.

Being a mama's boy has proved to be a very good thing.

Only some people can pull off wearing mulderaiken's Fugly jackets.

Blends Created By Bonnie Wallace

CHAPTER TWENTY-FIVE

A woman working in a Hong Kong hospital helping Sars
patients wrote—when she comes home each night from
dealing with the human carnage, she listens to Clay sing and
it helps sooth her weariness and helps her forget momentarily
of the harm that surrounds her.

NOTES AND QUOTES

Simon: "Why are you here?"
Clay: "Uh, I'm the *American Idol*."

Jan Mitchelle: "Clay has the innocence and charm of Opie,
the sex appeal of Elvis, the humor, stage presence and knack for
connecting with an audience of Billy Chrystal (with a few drops
of Billy Graham) all mixed together and gift-wrapped in the
voice of an angel."

Lynn Elber: "Clay and other '*American Idol*' contestants are
fond of the obscure fact that Gladys Knight was discovered on

Ted Mack's Amateur Hour. 'I would love to have that kind of history,' Aiken said, but diplomatically adds: 'I don't want to abandon that part of me (*American Idol*) because I wouldn't be here if not for that show.'"

Beautiful Girl Magazine: "While other teen magazines rank hot guys on what they look like, we've selected an amazing group of guys for Who they look up to," said publisher Scarlett Williams. "Our readers think that what makes a guy his hottest is his relationship with God like Clay has."

Mark Roberts: "Faye Parker, Clay's mother, has been at his side ever since he was just another face in the '*American Idol*' crowd. Life has changed for Clay, but it has also changed for her. She said, 'There are some times when I want to go in my house and shut the door and scream, 'Help, help!'"

Judy Simpson: ".... And, with God's grace, we witnessed the miracle that is Clay Aiken. When it comes to finding anyone who approaches the miracle that is Clay Aiken, frankly, I don't think "*American Idol*" has got a prayer."

Anne Sherber: "Walt Disney's... Aladdin... due on DVD.... '*American Idol*' winner Clay Aiken has recorded 'Proud of Your Boy,' a song Menken wrote with partner Howard Ashman... Menken... was thrilled to have the "opportunity to bring this song to life. 'Hearing Clay sing this song Howard and I wrote 17 years ago...I was emotionally blindsided,'" Menken said.

Jay Leno: "*American Idol* judge Randy Jackson is doing well after having gastric bypass surgery. He said his goal is to lose two Clay Aikens or half of a Ruben."

Clay: "I'm thrilled with all the success... with all the opportunities I've had. I just want to say to people... that it's not all limos and black-tie affairs. There are some parts that make me question, "Would I like to be a teacher again?" The answer sometimes is yes."

Bonnie Wallace

Ryan Seacrest: "Clay, do not pull Ruben's hair."
Clay: "I will try my best."

Associate Press: Clay said, "I try to remember it was just barely a year ago that I was... in North Carolina not doing much but teaching and going to class and turning my homework in late," And it could very easily come back to that at any moment...."

Faye Parker.: "Since Clayton has become one of the most famous men in America our life has been on a roller coaster.... I knew... that Clayton had been blessed by God with much talent. It is not ours to know what God plans to do with our lives. We each have a purpose and it is truly remarkable that at such a young age Clayton has been shown his."

Randy Jackson asked Clay What was the most memorable moment of his Idol experience?

Clay: "It... was going home and singing for my hometown on the tour and... being introduced for the first time in Raleigh.... I come from a medium-sized city that's got a small-town feel to it. The support that came out of that city was unbelievable, unexpected, and overwhelming."

Bios: "Clay Aiken, Ruben Studdard, Kelly Clarkston and other AI winners noticeably convey on-going appreciation to their fans. Clay acknowledged during the AI Tour that every city he performs in is a 'thank you' for his fans amazing support."

Clay: "I'm 24 and from Raleigh, North Carolina— (the audience cheers). "Oh, you're from Raleigh?" (To someone in the audience.) "Yesss! That's great, but if you're here, then who's back home?"

Frankie Muniz: "I think Clay is going to win!"

Clay: "I just want to change the world somehow."

Simon: "If I am telling the truth I think your a little off tonight." Then.... "I think that performance could win you this competition."

Clay: "I'm no different. I'm not different at all. The wrapping is different. The gift is the same."

Faye Parker's sign in the audience: Airfare: $300, Hotel: $100 a night, seeing my son Clay, become the next *American Idol*: PRICELESS!

Clay: "To see my name in lights has never really been a dream of mine. I'm perfectly happy teaching. I really, honest to God, I am."

Jaded Journalist: "So what are you gonna wear next week that'll look good?"
Clay: "Maybe I'll, I'll... do you have any advice for me? Some wing-tipped tennis shoes?"

Clay: "It's important that I make a difference in some way. It's not necessarily how I make a difference, but I want to make sure that I do."

Michael Felberbaum — The *Associated Press*: Clay ".... One of the lessons I have learned is that you can't make plans for yourself because God has surprises. One of the things I want to make sure is (the success of)...the Bubel Aiken Foundation.... Maybe in a few years... my hope is that the foundation will be able to be successful, and I can work on that."

Randy Jackson's book "What's Up Dawg," Clay said, "Being able to balance the time that I owe to the public, to the time I owe to myself is what I have found most difficult."

Clay: "What comes out of this is what God wants to happen."

TVtome.com: "...I think the voting from last night should be looked at under the world's biggest microscope. Because I smell a rat... for *American Idol* to maintain the credibility of it's premise (AMERICA VOTES) the crappola that played out tonight needs to be addressed."

Jaded Journalist: CA— "I'm sorry, am I hurting your feelings?"
JJ: "Yeah"
CA: "I'm sorry. No, really I'm not."
CA: "Because I'm from North Carolina, you think I'm the Andy Griffith show or something?"

Clay: "It's a pop-flavored album. I think there are a lot of people out there who may not be the best influence for kids. I wouldn't want my kids listening to some of the stuff out there. None of the stuff on the album is like that."

If you want to know about Clay Aiken's album and CD sales ask WNYClayfan and The Clayboard..

Nygel Lythgoe: "Simon has made no secret that he was not happy with the emergence of guest judges.... "The only time he's happy to be next to anyone is when he's leaning against a mirror."

Conan O'Brien: Kelly Clarkson—"Omgosh Clay is so funny! He is hilarious!"

Oprah: Clay— "I need to trust myself and do what is right for me. I want to make sure that I stay true to who I am."

Clay: "I think Ruben and I will always be linked together in everyone's minds. I think we're a pair now."

Us Magazine: Clay— "I didn't get cut tonight—I just didn't win"

Clay: "It's just odd, because I don't understand why people like me that much."

Rolling Stone: J. Levy— "Clay Aiken. An honest... bonafide where did that guy come from star?"

Faye Parker: "They think my sons a sex symbol. That's funny."

Clay: "Did you watch the show last night where this girl knew everything about me?"

On Air With Ryan Seacrest: Merv Griffin— "...Clay Aiken.... He's got energy. He's got soul. He's got it all...that voice pours out of him!"

Clay (about selling a multi-platinum album): "I can handle that."

Simon on EXTRA: "I think Clay and Ruben know that they're winning this competition."

Reporter: "Did any of the finalists have a habit that got on your nerves?"
Joshua Gracin: "Yea, Clay even sings in his sleep."

Clay: "I'm tired. I don't know what day it is."

Ryan: "You've won the sate of Ohio!"
Clay: "Well thank you, Ohio."

Clay: "I think there's a difference between appearance and image. An image is not how you look. It's what you do. It's what you portray. Your personality, the example you set, and that's huge for me."

Billboard: Clay— "I was born in Raleigh. Spent my whole life in Raleigh. Never left Raleigh until I did this show. Well, that's a little exaggerated."

Clay: "I'll be honest, when I got to the 'X-Men' premiere, and everyone's looking at me... and I'm on the front page of both the papers, there is a little bit of me that doesn't want it to stop.... After you've finally seen how cool it can be, it is kind of contagious."

Ruben : "Before I tried out, I thought this competition was really cheesy, but now look where I am!"
Clay: "The King of Cheese!"

Audience Question: "Clay, I know you've gotten rid of your glasses, gotten contacts, and changed your hair. Are you more comfortable with the image you have now or when you were a dork?"

Clay: (surprised) "Well, once a dork, always a dork! There are people who fix me up. They do my hair and pick out my clothes, which makes it much easier for me."

Clay: "I'm not different. I'm not different at all. The wrapping is different but the gift is still the same." (On his makeover.)

Ryan: "What do you have to say to Simon? I mean your just up there not taking yourself to seriously."
Clay: "I don't take him to seriously." (After Grease performance.)

Clay's definition of an *American Idol*: "American celebrities have an amazing amount of influence on the way America thinks, feels, and acts. I think that such an influence should be used in the most positive way possible."

Randy Jackson: "You're definitely one of the best in America. Gotta give it up."

Clay: "I enjoy singing and that's what I'm here to do. I know I'm not a model; I'm not going to be. I'm not the best lookin' person here, and that's fine. That's not what it's about to me."

Joshua Gracin: "I don't know for sure who will win this competition. But I do know, in my opinion who deserves to win... and that is Clay."

Clay: "Sometimes I feel really bad, like I took someone else's spot."

Jaded Journalist: Clay— "Well actually he said he prefers, he prefers me when his eyes are closed. He wasn't quite that harsh."

Bios: "Clay's endearing face of gratitude was evident when he stood before the 'American Idols Live!' crowd at the RBC Center in Raleigh North Carolina. Clay became emotional after singing, 'This Is The Night.' He stood with tears in his eyes for several minutes as fans screamed their approval for their local hero."

Newscaster: "Did your Mom fix you a nice warm breakfast?"
Clay: "The hotel gave me a muffin."

Regis and Kelly Live: Clay: "What are you talking about? I've always looked like this! But seriously, it takes many people working 24 hours around the clock to make me look like this!"
Kelly: "Welcome to my world!"

Clay: "I got a letter from a lady who said that she had a Clay Aiken pillowcase which frightened me to no end."

ET: Joshua Gracin— "I think with all the media surrounding him, Ruben will win. But deep down in my heart I feel that Clay should win."

Ryan: "What are you thinking about in this fan poster?"
Clay (looks at a Clay painting): "I think I may be sleeping. I think you can see my brains right up through my nostrils!"

Jaded Journalist: "Now we must all hide from Clay's obvious psychic powers when he said he would get to #1 or #2 at least!"

Motown Video: Clay— "It's important that I make a difference in some way. If it's performing and touching someone that way, that's great; If it's being a teacher and helping some kid under-stand something, that's even better. It's not necessarily how I make a difference, but I want to make sure that I do."

Paula Abdul: "Clay, this is what this competition is about. This is what the wild card is about—big fan, love you hair.... You've raised the bar.... You've surpassed the bar. You're a star and you've got this confidence about you that is quiet and subtle, that's not intimidating.... Great job."

Jaded Journalist: "Why don't you show us how you can turn your feet backwards?"

Kelly Rippa: "So what's it like with your makeover? I mean with the hair and the
Clothes...."

Clay: "When I look in the mirror, I see me."

The Raging Critic's: "Simon said this song MAY win you this competition. I will take Simon's words a little further and say that this song DID win you this competition!"

Clay: "I didn't get cut tonight; I just didn't win."

People Magazine: "I know that I've got big ears and a big forehead and that my hair sticks up, but I'm happy with myself. I'm not necessarily trying to win a beauty pageant here."

Clay: "There is a thrill that you get when you perform and everybody is cheering for you...This is the biggest audition that I've ever had."

Rolling Stone' Magazine: "I'm really not that special. Really, I'm not. It was just a T.V show."

Gladys Knight: "Your voice is so pure. I don't know what's going to happen for you in the contemporary world, but somewhere along the way something exceptional is going to happen for you because you're pure."

Album photo shoot: Clay: "I think I've broken three cameras

today."

Clay: "American celebrities have an amazing amount of influence on the way America thinks, feels and acts. I think that such an influence should be used in the most positive way possible."

Verdine White: "When I saw you backstage earlier, you didn't look like you could sing. But you can sing. You've got chops!"

Clay: "It's not the money. It's not the fame. It's the influence."

Nigel Lythgoe: "When he first walked in, let's face it, he looked like he had two satellite dishes growing out his head."

Clay: "There is nothing worse to me than a house cat. When I was about sixteen, I had a kitten and ran over it. Seeing that cat die, I actually think that its spirit has haunted me."

Clay: "Two weeks ago I was just a college student in North Carolina on the way to becoming a teacher and now my life has completely taken a different direction."

People Magazine: Clay— "I'm religious. I think this is something that God had planned for me."

Clay: "...as long as you're living right, then you don't have to worry about what people see."   (On the pressures of being in the public eye.)

Ryan: "Who says—Baby, Dude, Dawg, Man, etc.?"
Clay: "Randy?"
Ryan: "No, Simon."

Clay: "It's not the money. It's not the fame. It's the influence."

Bruce Barker "Thank God Clay Aiken side stepped the genre

and sang 'Ever Lasting Love' or I might have gone entirely insane"

Clay: "I try not to think about it as much as possible" (After being asked about being a sex symbol.)

Rolling Stone: "I've never minded being the sidekick, which is why coming in second place on *American Idol* is totally a non-issue for me.... If my first album flops, all I have to say is, what'd you expect? I didn't win.'"

Clay: "After I sang 'Somewhere Out There,' Simon said, 'You're the one to beat.' Getting a compliment from Simon is like getting water out of a rock."

Jaded Journalist: "Oh I see. I guess I heard it differently."
Clay: "Mm hmm." .... "Which is funny, because I prefer you when your mouth is closed."

Detroit News: Joshua Gracin— "Clay, hands down. He's the most dedicated, he's the most determined, and he's the most deserving.... I mean, he's never been off pitch, ever." (When Joshua was asked whom he thought would win.)

Clay: "I'm religious. I think this is something God had planned for me."

Simon Cowell: "I prefer you when I shut my eyes."

Clay: "I don't understand why people like me! It doesn't make any sense!"

Ryan Seacrest: "He's grown the most. Clay is this year's Kelly Clarkson"

Clay: "It was a comedy... I was in my pajamas.... We had 10

minutes to pack and get to the airport. Then we went to the wrong hanger, and Ruben had to use the bathroom, so we were falling behind. Then we were all in line putting everything into the plane. Takeoff time: 9:58 (airport had 10:00 curfew)."

Neil Sedaka: "I would kill to write and produce your first CD!"

Clay: "It's important that I make a difference in some way. If it's performing and touching someone that way, that's great; if it's being a teacher and helping some kid understand something, that's even better..."

Clay: "One of the first things I'm gonna do is set up a foundation. Since I'm not going to be teaching for a while, I'd still like to stay connected and use this platform to bring attention to autism awareness and to individuals with disabilities."

WRAL: Clay— "I haven't gotten to see my mom enough!"

Clay: "If god wants me to win, I'll win. I totally rely on him. If he wants me to come in 2nd place, then that's where I'll come in."

Idolonfox: "I enjoy singing and that's what I'm here to do..... I mean that photo shoot was a debacle.... They're like, 'Don't smile with your mouth open, you close your eyes when you do that'.... I'm not the best looking person here, and that's fine...."

Clay: "I left Raleigh six months ago, and nobody knew who I was. It's very hard to get used to."

Oprah: "Clay is turning into a real life rock star.... going to be on the cover of *Rolling Stone* Magazine. You know you've arrived when Rolling Stone Magazine asks you to grace their cover. A rite of passage reserved for rock and pop royalty."

Clay: "I'm six foot one...." "When you stand beside Ruben, you look short."

Ryan Seacrest: "These two gentlemen a step closer to being in the top 10 and Clay, still more nervous than ever. He asked me to pee three times in that break, and I said 'No, we're coming back in a second!'"

Clay: "We're extremely happy, cuz America didn't go with the image thing so much this year."

US Magazine: Clay— "Hopefully I'll have what Ruben has...except for the title."

Clay: "It's a whole team of people working 24 hours around the clock to make me look like this."

Jeff on Regis & Kelly: "Clay Aiken has left the studio! There's nothing we can do for you, folks!"

Clay: "I am who I am, God made me, and yeah, I could have done my hair a little bit better." (A fan asked him what he saw in the mirror)

Ryan: "Did you know that you've lost those facial expressions?"
Clay: "Yeah, I've worked on them.

Ryan: "Where do you work on stuff like that? At the house in the mirror?"
Clay: "Yeah. I don't know if I look in the mirror as much as you."
Ryan: "Probably not."

Clay: "They told us to sing a song by our idol. Well, my mother's really my idol, so I'm gonna sing her favorite song for me to sing— 'Unchained Melody' by the Righteous Brothers."

Oprah— "Ruben you were said you didn't care much that you were in the bottom 2."
Ruben— "I didn't but Clay was crying."

Clay: "Well, it's a British song, Simon." - Clay after he sang, "Build me Up Buttercup."

Rolling Stone Magazine: "Either you're a womanizer, or you've got to be gay.... since I'm neither... people are like totally concerned about me. There like 'What are you then'"?

Clay: "An image is not how you look. It's what you do. It's how you portray your personality, the example you set."

"Trenyce honey, are you ok?" Clay at the X2 Premiere.

Clay: "I'm really not that special. Really, I'm not. I was on a big TV show, but it was just a TV show."

The Pulse: Clay— "These (indicates his ears) are gonna be here forever. So they're big! I don't mind."

Clay: "You might not can tell by looking at us, but we are kind of different."(Smiling, regarding his relationship with Ruben Studdard.)

Paula Abdul: "Clay you are a true artist, because you sang a classic song and made us feel like we've heard it for the first time."

Clay: "I'm tired and I don't know what day it is."

Simon "Everything about that was horrible." (Indicating Clay's Grease performance.)

Oprah: "Clay's voice makes his fans melt—a lot. Get out the ice cubes and see for yourself."

Clay: "I never knew that people made a club for me!"

Idolonfox: Clay—"It's kinda surreal you know, cause I didn't think I'd get this far.... I mean this is big, the bottom 32.... It's kinda like... the Miss America Pageant. Everybody's been so nice, and very supportive."

US Magazine: Clay— "I never thought I'd be an object of affection!"

Clay: "There's nothing so wrong that it can't be easily fixed or easily ignored, I just let things roll off."

Clay: "Getting used to (my new contact lenses). I'm sure I was looking at Randy once when Paula was talking."

Oprah: Clay— "I'm slowly getting used to a lot of this stuff. I don't really think of myself as a celebrity. I think of myself as the guy back from Raleigh, who just happened to have an amazing experience."

Clay: "Whenever we have free time I try to sleep."

Simon: "Wow! I was really impressed, and you know.... I think the fact that you don't look like a pop star...actually in a way is a good thing because you are so memorable and you're sort of looking better each week as well. It was great, really, really, great!" (After Clay's Wild Card performance.)

Clay: "I'm not going to unpack, I'm just going to live out of my suitcase. I don't want to get too used to being here."

To 'The Jaded Journalist': Clay— "Is this interview prepared at all, or it is fly by the seat of your pants?"

Priscilla Brame, Clay's teacher at the UNCC. "He came in my office and he told me he was going to do *American Idol* and I said, 'Clay can you sing?' He said, 'Yeah, I can sing.' And his friend Amy was with him and I said, 'Amy, can Clay sing?' And she said, 'Yeah, he can sing.'"

Clay: "Can I be the next bachelor?" "I never thought I'd be an object of affection. That's the biggest surprise of the whole experience!"

Ryan Seacrest: "Clay, how do you feel about all the money you are earning?"
Clay: "Well, you aren't gonna turn it down!"

Girl in the audience: "I love you, Clay"
Clay: "I love you too!"

"Clay, You are truly unique, and you are like our best friend on television that's how humble you are."

Disc Jockey, Java Joel: Joel teasingly sang a bar of 'Unchained Melody,' trying to get Clay to sing with him—Clay declined. Then, Joel asked Clay, "What is your favorite song to sing?" Clay replied, "Well, it was 'Unchained Melody' until you sang it!"

Amy E—"What a truly humble and amazing guy. No matter what happens, he will always have a fan in me. Thanks for giving us all a voice from Heaven and a wonderful role model for young people."

Bios: "Later before singing 'Invisible,' a song from his album, he again became emotional, introducing his mom to the crowd.

He said, his voice breaking, 'I would never be able in a thousand years to thank you for what you've done for me.'"

Kimberly Locke was asked why women are so crazy about Clay. She said, "He's the perfect man. Perfect in that he's thoughtful, responsible, socially and politically conscious, educated, affectionate and loving, sincere, has a huge heart, is giving and not to mention incredibly handsome with a golden voice."

Jaded Journalist: "So what's Clay short for Clayford, Claytaford?"
Clay: "Yeah, Claytina."
Jaded Journalist: "Both?"
Clay: "Mmmmhmm, Claytina."

Gladys Knight: "There's something magical about your look."
Audience Member: "He's SEXY!"
Paula: "Yeah, He's sexy!"

Simon: "You might as well end the competition now. You have to put your money on Clay. I just can't see anyone beating him at this point."

EW: Ruben— "Clay's my Dawg."
Clay: "Ruben hits me."

Gladys Knight: "You're a mystery. There's something very magical about your look."

AI: Clay— "Ryan, are you available?"
Ryan: "What? Would you please rephrase that?"
Clay: "Are you avail ... oh my goodness!"

An AI audience member ask Clay who he thought could play him in a movie:

Clay: "Um, how about that guy Yahoo Serious? I heard I kinda look like him"
Ryan: "How about someone like Brad Pitt?"
Clay: "Brad Pitt—ok Brad Pitt. He can play me in a movie."
Ryan: "That's a cocky choice, Clay!"

Randy: "Dude! Every week I say, 'Where does that voice come from—the power, the range'?"

Nat Lauzon: "I think women like stuffed animals because we are naturally drawn to cute, innocent, wide-eyed furry things, like kittens and bunnies and Clay Aiken."

Simon: "This show proves Randy Jackson hasn't got a clue what he's talking about because that song was perfect for you. Absolutely on the money. Well done."

AI: Ryan Seacrest— "Simon said that it was sweet, but you sounded the same as last week. Well apparently sounding the same as last week suits them fine because you are safe."

Clay said most of assignments he handed in at UNNC were usually late.

Neil Sedaka: "Clay, you sing like Andre Agassi plays tennis— Perfection. Perfection!"

Simon asked Clay what Buttercup meant.
Clay: "Buttercup is a person, a pet name."
(Women in Audience): "Build me up, Clay!!"

Paula Abdul: "I think you're gorgeous, adorable and so freak- ing talented!"

Neil Sedaka: "Bravo Clay. I have lost my song forever to you. It will always be a Clay Aiken song."   Following Clay's

"Solitaire" performance.

Clay: "I think I've moved enough for the rest of the season. So, I'm going to calm down a little bit. I might break something, I think." Clay following his Grease performance.

Kimberly Locke: "And now after getting all this pampering, it's time to go back to work."
Clay: "I'm never going back to work."

Simon: "I think the best two are up there." (Indicating Clay and Ruben on the night of the finals.

Bios: "Those in charge of his career have finally caved in and said, 'Let Clay Be Clay.' Do you know why? They had no choice! Clay refuses to participate in "the dark side" of enter-tainment."

Clay: "I think the people who did the best on the show were the people who had the best sense of ... this is about winning and... about competing. Yes, I'm going to have fun... make some friends. It's going to be a neat experience... here with a purpose—to get the job done."

Laura: "I haven't been this giddy about a singer since Paul McCartney when I was 10."

B.B: "The contest is over, but the results will always be suspect."

Clay: "Well, it's a British song, Simon." - Clay after he sang, "Build me Up Buttercup."

Clay: "While I may have this jersey on, clearly I'm not an athlete, so I need y'all to pray... that this ball gets all the way over to home!" (Clay before throwing the opening pitch in

Raleigh at the Durham's Game.)

Bios: "I am surprised Music Corporatists' haven't caught on earlier. Maybe they have been too busy suing a 12 year old and 65 year old for "music pirating," because they downloaded some music off the Internet, that was available to download."

Simon Cowell: "The competition would not have been the same without Ruben."

Jaded Journalist "... Clay comes out and... he's serious about tonight because he's put on the jacket and tie and is now making his hair glow. Or maybe that's just the lighting.... Clay's hair is glowing again. So maybe it isn't the lights. Maybe it's Clay's magical powers!"

Kelly Rippa: "Now Clay, is it true that many of your fans don't actually own phones?"
Clay: "Yeah, they just scream to their neighbors who they want to win."

Clay: "Getting a compliment out of Simon is like getting water out of a rock"

Erin: "What this girl needs now ... is Clay, sweet Clay ... He's the only one who makes my day."

Time: Aiken said, "They (the music industry) don't understand the reasons that someone as uncool as me is here. In a way...it's a revolution." The Claymates have picked up the "REVOLU-TION" theme and are promoting it all over the internet. The swell for decency is growing."

B.B: "Clay needed protection from the same degradation Simon used to unmercifully beat up Trenyce—the contestant with the dazzling voice who deserved greater appraisal than his drag dirt."

Clay: "That's 130,000 people I'm going to have to beat up after the show." (He lost *American Idol* by 130,000 votes.)

"Clay indicated that autistic kids would try anything imaginable to try and communicate because communication to them is a conundrum."

Clay's friend Amy said Clay hardly ever studied for tests. She would be stressing over a test and he'd say that he wasn't going to worry about it, and he would just wing it and he got decent grades.

Alisha Puckett: "He still enjoyed (singing) for children at hospitals and for the elderly at Christmas and that was why God had blessed him with such an awesome talent — not to make six figures and live in a recording studio."

Bios: "Clay said he loved his napping couch. His couch? Maybe it's the cherry red sofa almost purchased by an fan who volunteered to max out her credit card (until Clay's mother discouraged it) and was ready to ship the suede sofa to Raleigh, North Carolina because she heard CA loved red. The scarlet love affair conjured up, was not from Clay. His favorite color is green— it was from his *American Idol* performance when he wore the hot red leather jacket when he whipped his greased hips and his fans into hysteria."

People Magazine: "Clay is the most improved...They set out to degeekify him and did a great job...."

B.B: "The results of his exposure to over 33 million people who have fallen in love with his humble demeanor and by his incredible voice have been overwhelming to this Raleigh Carolina school boy. He just can't figure it out, because all he ever wanted to be was to be a school teacher and help children."

Larry King Live: Clay— "...it's...hard to get used to because... all of us were kind of thrown into the fire. We became some-what household names really quickly, within a matter of ... three or four months.... It's really...hard to understand....I can't imagine that people actually like me."

Oprah: "You know you've made it when you only need one name, like Madonna or Celine, to make fans go wild.... It's 'The Voice' that will keep Clay's star shining."

Clay: "Don't worry, I'll beat him up after the show for stealing my title!" (After losing AI to Ruben.)

"Nobody has been more surprised from the massive attention than Clay Aiken!!"

UNCC's Professor Cheryl Young said about Clay Aiken. "He is perhaps one of the smartest people I know."

Bios: In response to his "I can't believe that people actually like me," comment on Larry King live. "That is an interesting state-ment coming from a young man who has women groveling to touch him and from men who think he is just plain phenomenal. However, if you wind the clock back four months before he tried out for *American Idol* there is different side of the coin toss. He was a fiery, sometimes dyed, red headed, rumbled be speckled kid who could hardly muster up a date. But that muster has turned into mass hysteria from women around the globe."

Clay: "I could not pick between Ruben and me. Oh. Yeah, I could. I'd pick me."

Randy Jackson: "Yo, Clay, man. I'm just sittin' here laughin' man... I'm havin' a good time tonight man. I liked that you were up there doin' your dance stuff, dawg. I like the moves, baby!" (After Clay's Grease performance.)

Larry King: Clay— "We... start the tour in July, and.... that's gonna be tough work, 39 cities throughout the county between July and August." (In reference to the *American Idol* Tour.)

Rolling Stone: Joe Levy— "He could have connected with an audience if he'd been working the drive-through at Burger King."

Blends Created By Bonnie Wallace

CHAPTER TWENTY-SIX

It is not every question that deserves an answer.

SYRUS

WHAT FANS WANT TO KNOW

If you were invisible what would you do?

Do you keep disguises hidden in your car?

What was your favorite Independent Tour Moment?

What was your favorite Solo Tour Moment?

Has there been someone in the audience that you would have like to meet?

Who has been greatest influence in your singing career?

Would you like to be in love?

Do you believe in soul mates?

Do you believe there is someone for everyone?

How old do you think you will be when you marry?

What was your favorite *American Idol* moment?

Who was your favorite male contestant on *American Idol*?

What do you really think of Simon Cowell?

What do you really think of Paula Abdul?

What do you really think of Randy Jackson?

What would you do if fame left without notice?

Other than your mother who is your greatest influence?

What size shoe do you really wear—12 or 13?

How did you feel when you stood in front of Simon each week, knowing what was coming?

Have you bought a house yet?

Where would you gradually like to settle down and live?

How long do you think your career will last?

You say you are a realist not an optimist. What do you see in your future?

How do you feel when you are introduced and you hear all the screaming?

Are you happy with your life choices, so far?

What would you change if you had a magic wand for a day?

How many kids do you think you will have?

Is there anything you would like to change in your past?

What are your favorite websites?

Who is your favorite country western star?

Who is your favorite gospel singer?

Do you believe in a life after this life?

Do you believe we are destined for God's work?

Do you believe your incredible fame was helped by a higher power?

Do you personally answer fan letters?

2222

222

Gaye Deamer

Do you think it's odd to have so many middle age women swooning over you?

Have you ever met someone you would like to spend more time with?

Do you have instincts on how to make a song your own?

Do you believe in love at first sight?

On Thanksgiving what is your favorite dessert?

What is your favorite Christmas meal?

Who house trained Raleigh?

How long did you have your pet Goat?

What kind of shampoo do you use?

What kind of deodorant do you use?

What's in your glove compartment?

What is the best gift you have ever received?

Do you still sing in your sleep?

Do you still sing in the shower?

If you could be someone else for just one day, who would that be?

Do you like hugging or kissing best?

228

How old were you when you had your first kiss?

Who was the first girl you had a crush on?

Did you mean it when you told Carmen Rasmussen to hurry and grow older so you could get married?

Do you do your own washing?

Do you still have people dress you?

If you could go back and relive one event what would it be?

Who was your best friend in High School?

Who was your best friend in College?

What is your favorite striped shirt?

What was your favorite moment on *American Idol*?

What do you think your next career move will be?

When did gain your faith?

What is your testimony on Christianity?

Will you always remain a Southern Baptist?

What is your greatest blessing?

Who is your favorite relative?

What was the scariest dream you've ever had?

What is your favorite movie?

What would your dream girl be like?

Is it a burden having so many women crazy over you?

What is the hardest thing about being so famous?

Do you have insomnia, or do you fall asleep when your head hits the pillow?

What is your greatest asset?

What brings you the greatest joy?

What makes you the saddest?

Since you're allergic to mint what kind of toothpaste do you use?

Do you pray daily?

Do you still bless your food in public?

What is your favorite vegetable?

What is your favorite fruit? And don't say Krispy Kreme doughnuts?

What behavior do you dislike in others?

What do you see as your future?

If you weren't a celebrity and you couldn't teach what would you pursue?

What has been the most humbling experience in becoming a star?

What fan has touched you the most?

What is the most irritating thing a fan has done?

What is your fondest childhood memory?

What is your worst childhood memory?

If you could live in any decade what would it be?

What is the worst illness you have ever had?

What has been your most devastating loss?

What has been your greatest surprise?

What main things do you always pack in your suitcase?

What is the most embarrassing moment in your life?

What has been your weirdest disguise?

Where has been the strangest place that people have recognized you?

As a celebrity what is the next thing you'd like to experience?

What was your best experience touring with Kelly Clarkston?

What was your worst experience touring with Kelly Clarkson?

If you could be the sponsor of any other foundation what would it be?

What actor or actress would you like to act with?

If you were the President, how would you change the world?

What is your political affiliation?

Have you ever met Fake Clay?

Would you like Kim Locke to be more than just a friend?

If you could have a perfume line what would you name it?

What would you love a girl to do to get your attention?

What are the main traits you will look for in a wife?

What is your favorite sport?

Have you ever had a desire to play a particular sport well?

If your face could be on any product what would it be?

What do you think of Jimmy Kimmel now that he has tried to mend the rift?

If you could judge Simon Cowell what would you say to him?

What suntan lotion do you use?

What aftershave do you use?

Do you shave with an electric shaver or a blade?

What is the best present you have ever received?

What is the worst present you have ever received?

Who would you like to play you in a movie?

If you could be in a comic book who would you like to be?

If you could have anyone in your music video who would you choose?

What other TV shows would you like to be on?
What's your e-mail address?

Do you like wearing a beard?

What do you eat for breakfast?

What is your favorite meal?

Do you peruse the Clay boards—which are your favorites?

Do you know what Tookie means?

What is your screen name?

What state would you like to live in?

What is your favorite genre of music-gospel or country?

What is the greatest thing your mother ever taught you?

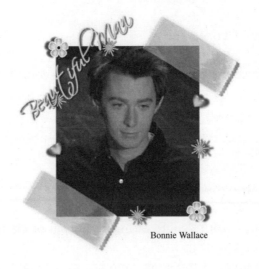

Bonnie Wallace

CHAPTER TWENTY-SEVEN

Kindness gives birth to kindness.

SOPHOCLES

FANS SEND MESSAGES TO CLAY

Oh Clay, you blow me away. I can't even begin to tell you how much I love you. You inspire me and show me that dreams really do come true. Thank you so much for letting us live this vicariously through you. Much love, Emily Loos

Clay the world needs more positive, Christian, admirable role models like you. I admire and adore you. XOXO Love, Brittney Rodee

Bonjour, I love you so much Clay Aiken! You are the angel in my night; you are the idol of my life. Nancy 1968

You are the new Barry Manilow. Thank you, Becky Messer

Clay, we (I) love ya, and if I could talk to you, I'd tell you why we middle-aged women are crazy about you. I hope fame never tarnishes your faith. I truly look forward to hearing you sing praises to Jesus In Heaven. Your voice is so pure now; I can't even imagine what you will sound like then. I'm not even your mom, but I am so proud of you for all your accomplishments. Stay true to yourself and your faith. God bless you. With much love. Belinda Adolfsen

Clay, never forget your roots. Always seek God first. If you seek Him you will find him. Keep looking to the stars you are a real winner and from what I can tell a real role model for children. I love your gentle spirit. I am praying for your success. Nancy6

Dear Clay, I am a major fan of yours. My mom, my daughter and I are always singing your songs. I love you because you are not afraid to be yourself. Just don't forget the children who need you. Love always your fan, Stacie Durrans

Dear Clay, I am a 70-year-old lady from Salt Lake City and I watched you on *American Idol* every week. I love you for your wholesome role model for others, and for the love you show your Mom. I wish you the best in your career. Always you fan, Joyce Carter

"God Sent"!! I knew the moment I saw Clay—I loved his voice.... Praise the Lord for wildcard rounds. I now know another reason why I love Clay; HE A CHRISTIAN — a Familiar spirit.... We will be praying for him that he stays the wonderful way he is in this secular world.... Our family can't wait for your new album to come out. We hope there's a Christian one coming soon. Marenisco

Clay, I hope my sons turn out to be just like you. Thank you for being such a good example. Your voice is amazing. Lisa M. Shepherd

Bonnie Wallace

Clay, I'm old enough to be your mom. I'm so impressed with your accomplishments. Keep your values that are impressive. Sally Haslam

Clay, you are an inspiration to us all! You are such a great example and such a great person. Thanks for all the memories. Jessica Goddard

Clay, I think that you are amazing!! I admire how you have remained your true self and haven't changed for the world. Thanks so much for being my idol. Jennifer Johnson

Clay! You are so amazing! We love your music and your talent! You're in our CD Player 24/7! Keep up the great work! Connie, Deanna, McKenzle and Jenn.

Dear Clay... I continue to be amazed with your voice, your character, and the sweetness of your ways. I am a very dedicated fan and bend over backward to go to your site and request your songs on my local radio station every single day. I have bought t-shirts and bumper stickers. I also have my walls totally pasted over with your face!! It makes me cry every time I hear your sweet voice. And if you are reading this Clay, I LOVE YOU! From I LOVE YOU.

Clay, I am so amazed by you and your accomplishments. You are a wonderful example and I wish everyone was like you. I love your voice. You are my *American Idol*. Jamie Johnson.

Clay, I saw your concert in Salt Lake City and I want to say that I Love You! Aubrey Messer

Clay, I voted and voted and voted for you. I knew your talent was something America was just waiting for. Thanks for sharing and staying true to who you are. Margaret Rodee

Good Luck Clay in everything you do. You're going to be a big star for many years to come.
You'll Always have a place in my heart, cause that's where I keep my valuables! Craftylady

Clay, You are truly the *American Idol*. I can't believe with all this fame you are still so humble and so down to earth. We Love You. Olivia Shepherd

Clay. You are so awesome, talented and genuine....May you go far and don't let success spoil you. Linda from Utah

Clay. You have gorgeous eyes. Not only are they beautiful to look at, but they radiate a goodness. More importantly that comes from your soul. Rebecca Bierwolf

.... Clay, you are so incredibly talented and have a genuinely amazing voice...I get chills every time I hear your singing, it's just flawless... you are the ideal role model. I think it is just so awesome how you are motivated to help others in need and to set good examples....You are the definition of '*American Idol*' and I think your hair is way cooler than Ryan Seacrest's. nd214

Clay. You are my one true inspiration with your heavenly voice. You are an angel. I will be falling to sleep listening to your voice forever. Love always, Jennifer Kendall

Clay. You're the best!! I love the album and I never missed the show. Shawn Gordon

Clay Baby!! You Rock! I love you!! Julie Gordon-Preston

Clay, Your singing inspires me and "lift(s) me up". I am truly moved whenever I listen to your single. Keep it coming. Can't wait for your new album(s). celine88

Clay. You are amazing. I love your voice. You have an outstanding gift. Mandy Batt

Clay. I love you. You have a way about you that's just soo adorable! I love watching you. You literally light up the stage. When you sing I melt of love, love. Love you tons, Michelle Bierwolf.

Clay. I love the example you are to young and old. Thanks, Debbie

Clay. You are da bomb! You so should be the *American Idol*! Good luck. Leslie Gregory

Dear Clay, Thank you for your inspiration and beauty and for helping me through a very difficult time. You are truly amazing! Love, Suzanne Brimall

Clay. I love your music. I think you are amazing. I think it is great that you don't care what the world thinks. Always stay true to who you are. Love Chelsea Bigler

.... I would love to meet you one day, but I am so shy. I am married, with 3 children.... I know you are confused by all this attention, but you have come out of hiding! We didn't know you before. Now that I am aware you exist, I'm excited! You are refreshing!! My best wishes to you, Clay. You are an inspiration! Alana A.

Clay. I think you are a great singer and I admire you. Miss Lewis and Amelia Nagle

Clay. From the mom of an autistic five year old. THANK YOU! Shalia Overbaugh

Clay. You are beautiful and so is your voice. Cassie Batt

I'm 62, just love to hear clay— sing keep up the good work. Shelbrajea

Clay. You are so cool! You have an amazing voice. Just don't become stuck up! Kassandra Egeland

Clay. When I first saw you, I LOVED YOU!! I love your voice and your attitude. Love Andrea Thompson, Age 12.

Clay. I just wanted to let you know that your voice is gorgeous. I just turned 21 Aug. 20, 2003 and you made my birthday a very happy one. I love you. Randi Vought

Clay. You are the Sunshine in a world full of clouds. Thank you for being a bright spot. Love Always! Katie Partridge

Clay you say you just want to make a difference whether it be singing or teaching. Clay you have already made a difference — you've brought great joy with your magnificent voice to all of your fans. When I listened to you I feel this sudden elation at just the sound of your voice. You are blessed with a wonderful gift and I know you will return this blessing to all that love you. Never change a thing about your singing of your values. Lvmfn

Clay. Hi, my name is Jessica LeClair Hudgins. I am 16 years old. I loved you the moment I first saw you. You are so, so cute and so, so nice. I know you won't let fame go to your head. I watched the show every single week and I voted for you the entire calling time each Wednesday. I love you, Jessica. YOU ROCK!

Clay. You are awesome. I loved you right from the start. You are my *American Idol*. Jan

Clay. You are the *American Idol* in my opinion. Good luck on your career. Diana

Clay. You are the best ever! You have done an amazing job! Your voice is ABSOLUTELY incredible. I listen to you all the time. Love you, Janie Thurgood

Thank you Clay for wearing the WWJD bracelet on the cover of *Rolling Stone*. Klaytina

Clay. You are such a cutie. You have such a good voice. You're my number #1 fan. Rachel Batt

Clay. You have been so inspiring to me. I have had a lot of medical problems this summer and your songs have gotten me through. I had eye surgery last week, but I am here at the concert here in Salt Lake to see you. Thank you so much, Lorie Eggleston

Clay. You are such a great guy! And you are truly my *American Idol*! Good luck in all you do. Xxxoooo, Love, Teresa Kendall

Clay. Thank you so much! You have inspired me SO much to

go farther and to always be better. Always be humble and happy! Thanks again, Trevor Dean

We love you Clay. Xxx000, Shirleen and Wesley

Clay, you are my *American Idol*. I have your tape and enjoy listening to it more each time I put it on... please do take care of your voice. We want you around for a long, long time. Elsie Hill

Clay. We love you. You are awesome. I love your voice. I am so excited just to be at your concert.. Love Diane Kropf

Clay. You are so awesome. Your voice rocks and you are just so comfortable on stage. That is an inspiration to me. Keep rocking. Scott Blackhurst.

Thank you, Clay, for never compromising who you are for doing the 'easy' thing! I've seen some discussion of age here. I'm 77 years old and no young person could love him more. He's on my desktop and when I turn my 'puter on in the morning, he smiles at me and I say 'good morning, Clay, I hope your day is a happy one'! There's no barrier love can't erase! Valuci

We love you Clay. Jack and Bethie

Steph E: "There have been many discussions about how Ruben is more 'marketable' than Clay...and in a way he is...because you would have to market Ruben. Clay markets himself, and we love him without gimmicks or special nicknames."

Steph's Mom: "I want him for my son-in-law."
Steph: "I want him for your son-in-law too."

CHAPTER TWENTY-EIGHT

The best of all the preachers are the men
who lives their creeds.

EDGAR A. GUEST

HOW TO FIND CLAY AIKEN?

WELCOME TO THE WORLD OF CLAY AIKEN

WELCOME TO CYBERSPACE

The questions fly—How can I find him? Where is he? What is he doing? These inquisitive fans (young and older) are most likely new to the Computer—the magical International Highways—of Information. Or some fans are just newly Clayed. You will discover he is as close as your mouse. Go to Search and type Clay Aiken. Hundreds of Thousands of entries are listed. Take your pick.

Here are samples (a myriad of great Clay Aiken sites) most

sites are not included—there are just so many. These are just a handful of possibilities:

THE OFFICIAL CLAY AIKEN SITE
URL: http://www.clayaiken.com

THE CLAYBOARD:
URL: www.claytonaiken.com

BOLT
URL:www.bolt.com

THAT'S THE CLAY
URL: www.thatstheclay.com

RED HOT TOPIC (RHT)
URL:www.redhottopic.com

CLAY AIKEN ONLINE
URL:http://www.clayaikenonline.com

THE AIRPLAY CENTRAL
URL: http://www.airplaycentral.com

THE IDEAL IDOL
URL: http://clayaikentheidealidol.com

SIR LINKS A LOT
URL: http://sirlinksalot.net/

AIKEN 4 YOU
URL: http://www.aiken4you.com/

CLAY MANIAC
URL: http://www.claymaniac.com/

THE PEOPLE'S REPUBLIC OF CLAY
URL: http://p083.ezboard.com/bthepeoplesrepublicofclay

LECHEROUS BROADS FOR CLAY AIKEN
URL:http://lbfca.diaryland.com/

ALL ABOUT AIKEN (AAA)
URL: http://pub156.ezboard.com/ballaboutaiken

MEASURE OF A FAN
URL: www.measureofafan.com

The CLAY TRAIN CONNECTION
URL: http://www.theclaytrainconnection.com/

ALL THINGS CLAY AIKEN
URL: http://www.allthingsclayaiken.com/index.html

Another avenue for discovery: Go to any search engine (e.g.—
Google) Type: Finding Clay Aiken. Again, the entries are infinite—you will not be disappointed. Or go to www.finding-
clayaiken.com. Here are the categories: Have fun:

WEBSITES (bios/news/pics/forums/mp3s/etc)
MESSAGE BOARDS (talk, talk, talk)
INDUSTRY/MEDIA (Clay fan areas)
PROMOTE CLAY (airplay/sales/fan help
PHOTOS/ART
MUSIC/MEDIA (downloads)
CHARITY/SERVICE/GOOD DEEDS
YAHOO CLAY GROUPS (rotated quarterly)
CLAY AND....
MERCHANDISE
FAN FICTION
FUN/MISC.
PRAYER/CHRISTIANS
MSN GROUPS
FANLISTINGS
FRIENDS OF CLAY

OR— go to Yahoo—There are 355 different groups of fans for Clay:
URL: http//groups.yahoo.com (type in Clay Aiken).

 MSN and other major websites also have similar clusters of fans. The results are amazing because...
Clay Aiken is everywhere— ENJOY!!

BIBLIOGRAPHY

BOOKS:

Cowell, Simon. "I Don't Mean To Be Rude, But..." Broadway Books, 2003

Jackson, Randy. "What's Up Dawg?: How To Become A Star In The Music Business." Hyperion, 2003

TELEVISION AND RADIO:

WRAL 5 TV. Ongoing Coverage, Starting November 2002 to Present

ABC "Jimmy Kimmel Live." June 28, 2004

NEWS 14 CAROLINA. "Aiken Takes To The Ice At The RBC Center." February 4, 2004

ABC "Nightline" Ted Koppel— February 2, 2004

NBC "Tonight Show" Jay Leno—January 21, 2004

ABC "Good Morning America" Diane Sawyer/Charles Gibson—October 22, 2003

CBS "Entertainment Tonight." October 22, 2003

ABC "Access Hollywood." October 22, 2003

ABC "The View" October 17, 2003

CBS "Early Show" October 17, 2003

ABC "Good Morning America" Diane Sawyer/Charles Gibson—October 15, 2003

MTV "TRL" October 14, 2003

CNN "Headline News." October 14, 2003

TVG "TV Guide Channel." October 14

NBC "Tonight Show" Jay Leno—October 13, 2003

ABC "Primetime" Diane Sawyer—October 9, 2003

NICK "Let's Just Play." October 4, 2003

ABC "20/20" John Stossell—Give Me A Break." October 3, 2003

CNN "CNN Live Today." August 13, 2003

ABC "The View" July 30, 2003

E! "E! News Live." June 16, 2003

ABC "Oprah." June 10, 2003

CTV "Canada AM." June 3, 2003

G4 Network "The Pulse." May 29, 2003

ABC "Live With Regis And Kelly." May 28, 2003

ABC "Good Morning America." May 28, 2003

NBC "The Today Show." May 26, 2003

CNN "Larry King Live." Larry King. "Dynamic Duo," May 24, 2003

CBS "The Early Show." May 22, 2003

ABC "Access Hollywood." May 21, 2003

FOX "AI Press Conference." May 21, 2003

FOX "Good Day Live." May 20, 2003

CBS "Entertainment Tonight." May 19, 2003

CBS "Extra." May 19, 2003

E! "E News Live" May 19, 2003

ABC "Oprah." May 13, 2003

MICROSPACE. "Makin' Aiken Happen Behind The Scenes" May 16, 2003

Your Weekend With Jim Brickman. "Clay Aiken Interview." June 26-27, 2004

Z100 NY. "Clay Aiken Interview." February 5, 2004

Kiss 98.5-Buffalo. Janet Snyder and Nicholas Picholas. New York, January 29, 2004

Sweet 98.5. Pat and JT In The Morning Show. Omaha, January 29,2003

Mix 101.5 WRAL FM. Bill and Sherry In The Morning. Raleigh, December 2003

94.1 FM . Jagger and Kristi. San Diego, Calif. October 2003

E! TV. "Clay Aiken Shaking American Pop." September 21, 2003

107.9 The Link. Matt and Ramona. Charlotte, North Carolina. July 1, 2003

Launch Radio Networks. "Clay Aiken Fans Claim '*American Idol*'s Results Fixed." July 12, 2003

Canada AM. Seamus. "Interview With Touring Idols." July 22, 2003

95.7 WLHT. Dave and Geri. Grand Rapids, Michigan.

MAGAZINES:

Lensch, Tonya and Schork, Robert. "Idol Worship." Reality Check, February 2004

Cooper, Chet and Melendres, Jennifer "Clay Aiken Interview." Ability Magazine, January 2004

Staff Writer "14 Questions For Clay" J-14, January 2004

Staff Writer "The Wrong Idol" J-14, January 2004

Cover Story. (Photographs, Mathias Clamer). "Clay Aiken— Revenge Of The Nerd." Teen People, December 2003— January 2004

Hiltbrand, David. "Do We Really Need Dueling '*American Idol*' Books?" Philadelphia Inquirer, Daily Magazine.

December 2003.

Macpherson, Andrew—photographer. "Clay Aiken." People (Sexiest Men Issue.) December 8, 2003

Svetkey, Benjamin, also Endelman, Michael "All Eyes On Britney." Entertainment Weekly, November 21, 2003

Seibel, Debra Starr. "And Now For Their Next Act." TV Guide, November 22-28, 2003

Staff Writer. "Has Clay Found His Miss Right?" In Touch, November 10, 2003

Flashback. "My Name is Clay Aiken." Teen People, November 2003

Glock, Allison. "Aching For Aiken." Elle, October 2003

Bronson, Fred. "Clay Aiken 'Measures Up On RCA Debut." Billboard, October 2003

Rozsa, Lori and Wang, Cynthia. "Feat Of Clay." People, October 20, 2003

Karger, Dave. "And The Geek Shall Inherit The Earth." Entertainment Weekly, P. 28-32, September 5 2003.

Ausiello, Michael. "Showdown Scrapped." TV Guide, July 19,2003

Hedegaard, Erik. "New Kid On The Block." Rolling Stone, July 10, 2003

Cover Story. "Who Really Won?" (P. 12-16.) In Touch, June 9, 2003

NEWSPAPERS AND WIRE RELEASES

Borden, Jeremy. "Singer Helps Y Launch Program." Charlotte Observer, June 24, 2004

Bream, Jon. "Aiken's Star Quality Shines In St. Paul." St. Paul Star Tribune, April 17, 2004

Hubbard, Rob. "Clay Finding Way; Kelly May Go Another." Pioneer Press, April 17, 2004

Eisele, Robert. "Kelly Clarston and Clay Aiken." Kansas City Star, April 16, 2004

Brown, Mark. "Live Singing At Concert—Who Would Have Thunk It?" Rocky Mountain News, April 14, 2004

Jordon, Isamu. "Kelly, Clay Delight Arena Crowd." Spokesman, April 10, 2004

Associated Press. "Idol Duo Get Crowd's Vote At Key Arena." Seattle Times, April 10, 2004

Stout, Gene. "Hearts Were Achin' For Clay Aiken Thursday Night At Key Arena." Seattle Post, April 10, 2004

Selvin, Joel. "A Runner-up Proves His Princely Worth." San Francisco Chronicle, April 9, 2004

Gonzales, Sandra. "Clarkston Is Just Fine, But Aiken Shines At 'Idol' Show." Mercury News, April 6, 2004

Kragen, Pam. "Clay And Kelly, A Study In Contrasts." NC Times, April 5, 2004

Wener, Ben. "Powerhouse duo Show Promise-Stepping Away From Their 'Idol' Start, Kelly Clarkston and Clay Aiken Display Big Potential At Pond Concert." The Orange County Register, April 5, 2004

Cromelin, Richard. " 'Idols' Are Human, But Louder—Though Clarkston's and Aiken's Limitations Are Evident, Screaming Things Adore The Show." L.A. Times, April 4, 2004

Hicks, Tony. "Surprise: Aiken Has Talent." Contra Costa Times, April 3, 2004

Evans, Will. "Clay Aiken's All The Craze At Arco In 'Idol' Love Fest." Sacramento Bee, April 2, 2004

Eyre, Jessica. "Aiken, Clarkston Wows Fans At Delta Center." The Daily Herald, March 29, 2004

Iwasaki, Scott. "Clay Aiken—High Note Of Show. Kelly Clarkston Sings Well But Without Spark." Deseret News, March 31, 2004

Deknock, Jan. "Sound System Drowns Kelly's, Clay Talent." Omaha World Herald, March 24, 2004

Klein, Joshua. "Humility and Charisma Distinguish 'Idol' Aiken." Chicago Tribune, March 23, 2004

Gilbert, Barry. "American Idols." St. Louis Dispatch, March 22, 2004

Quinn, Erin. "Clarkston Eclipsed By Feats Of Clay." Star-Telegram, March 20, 2004

Atlas, Darla. The Dallas Morning News. March 19, 2004

Apple, Charity. "Aiken And Clarkston Excited Twin city Crowd On Saturday." Times-News, March 16, 2004

Pullen, Doug. "Clay Aiken Works His Way Into Heart Of 'Idol' Audience." The Flint Journal, March 12, 2004

Weinstein, Elizabeth. "One Idol Shines; Another Searches." The Columbus Dispatch, March 12, 2004.

Milbouer, Stacy. "A Telegraph Column." The Telegraph, March 11, 2004

Amatangelo, Amy. "Clarkston And Aiken Live Up To 'Idol'atry." Boston Herald, March 10, 2004

McLennan, Scott. "Idol Duo Breaking From Pack." The Telegram, March 10, 2004

Graham, Renee. "Bubbly 'Idol' Stars Give Concert Real Pop." Boston Globe, March 9, 2004

Stout, Alan K. "Singers Show There's Talent In 'Idol." Wilkes Barre, March 8, 2004

Lewis, Catherine P. "At MCI, American Idolatry For The Feats Of Clay And Kelly." Washington Post, March 8, 2004

Guzman, Rafter. "Still More Puppets Than Idols" Newsday, March 6, 2004

Aquilante, Dan. "Aiken Not Fakin: He's The Real Deal." New York Post, March 6, 2004

Menconi, David. "Aiken Was Best Of Two 'Idol' Stars." News Observer, March 2, 2004

Peltz, Jennifer. "Aiken and Clarkston Show Off Idol Mettle." Sun-Sentinel, March 1, 2004

Gershman, Rick. "Clay Soars, Kelly Rushes." St. Pete Times, Feb 28, 2004

Piccoli, Sean. "Devoted Fans Follow Feats Of Clay Aiken." Sun-Sentinel, Feb. 28, 2004

Ehlers, Matt. "Clay Hits the Road." The News Observer, February 27, 2004

Devores, Courtney. "Clay Shines In City He Calls Home." The Charlotte Observer, Feb. 25, 2004

Cohen, Howard. "Here He Comes, Mr. *American Idol*." The Miami Herald, February 27, 2004

Deggans, Eric. "America Loves A Runnerup." St. Petersburg Times-Floridian, February 26, 2004

Hay, Carla. "Clay Aiken—The 'Measure' Of A Rising Star." Washington Post also Billboard, February 21, 2004.

Breznican, Anthony. "Idol Creation Makes Fuller A Fortune." Miami Herald, January 14, 2004

Murray, Sonia. "Musical Chairs In The Record Industry." The Atlanta Journal-Constitution, February 4, 2004

"Idol' Star Aiken Returns To Alma Mater." Associated Press, January 15, 2004

Ehlers, Matt. "This Was The Year For Aiken." News Observer, December 31, 2003

St. Petersburg Times. "Idol Star Aiken Awarded Degree." December 22, 2003

Petrozzello, Donna. "'Idol' Hosts No Idol Hand." New York Daily News, December 3, 2003

Graff, Gary. "Feat Of Clay." Oakland Press (Detroit), October 12, 2003

Rowell, Rainbow. "Idol Star Strikes Chord With Fans." World Herald, October 8, 2003

Rose Elaine. "They Came For Pomp, Pageantry And Clay Aiken." Press of Atlantic City,
September 21, 2003

Wener, Ben. "Pop Life." The Orange County Register, September 1, 2003

Braxton, Greg. "Fan-Pandering Antics Rev Up 'Idol' Showcase." LA Times, September 2-03

Spanberg, Erik. "N.C. Happy For, If Bemused By, Its Idol." Christian Science Monitor, August 15, 2003

Pierce, Scott D. "Aiken Steals The 'Idols Live' Show." Deseret News, August 25, 2003.

Dyer, Leigh. "Famous Runner-Up Learns To Sing To Screaming Audiences." Charlotte Observer, August 9, 2003

Mah, Jackie. "Charlotte Screams For Clay-Idol Runner-up Brings Coliseum To Feet." Charlotte Observer, August 9, 2003

"*American Idol* Runner-Up Hits Hometown On Concert Tour."

Associated Press, August 6, 2003

Ehlers, Matt. "Clay Returns To Cheers." News Observer, August 7, 2003

"N.C.'s Clay Aiken Plays To Hometown Crowd." Associated Press, August 7, 2003

Barnes, Steve. "Idols Not Worthy Of Worship." Albany Times Union, August 5, 2003

Ehlers, Matt. "No Idols Before Clay." News Observer, August 3, 2003

Ruggieri, Melissa. "Idol Thoughts." Richmond Times Dispatch, July 31, 2003

Smith, Andy. "Being An *American Idol* Means A Lot Of Pressure." Providence Journal, July 31, 2003

Aronoff, Jen. "'Idol' Hands Do Their Work." Buffalo News, July 20, 2003

Berger, Arion. "Orchestrated 'Idols' With Real Live Fans." The Washington Post, July 30, 2003

Amatangelo, Amy. "Tour Review" Boston Herald, July 28, 2003

Hinds, Julie "Feat of Clay: Ruben Won '*American Idol*' So Why Is Clay Mr. Popularity?" Free Press, July 18, 2003

Stout, Alan K. "'Idol' Live Earns 8,000 High Marks." Wilkes Barre, July 17, 2003

Jenkins, Mandy. "Aiken Steals The Show." Cincinnati

Enquirer, July 15, 2003

Lindquist, David. "American 'Idols' Tour Improves From 2002." Indianapolis Star Review, July 13, 2003

Berkley. "Goofy, Gorgeous-The Many Faces Of Clay." Assistant Director Of Motion Pictures and Screenwriter. August 25, 2003

Pierce, Scott D. "Clay Aiken Steals 'The Idols' Live Show." Deseret News, August 25, 2003

Barker, Bruce. "Idol Chartwatch." Foxes On Idol." July 7, 2003

Bream, Jon. "Familiar Faces, Familiar Formula at 'Idol' Concert." St. Paul Star Tribune, July 9, 2003

Klein, Joshua. "*American Idol* Tour On A Roll." Chicago Tribune, July 10, 2003

Weiss, Tara. "Second Place Stardom. The Losers On television Reality Shows Are Turning Out To Be The Real Winners." Hartford Courant, July 4, 2003

Bayot, Jennifer. "Unlikely Pop Idol Sells Like The Real Thing." New York Times, June 7, 2003

Graybeal, Geoffrey. "I Don't Really Know Clay Aiken." The Herald Sun, May 20, 2003

Puckett, Alisha. "Clay who? Idol Finalist remembered As Class Clown." The Herald, May 21, 2003.

Dyer, Linda. "Autistic Teen's Family All Aiken Fans." Charlotte Observer, April 03, 2003

Berry, Wendi. The Herald-Sun, February 13, 2003

Below are Review Sources of AI Tour:

St. Paul Star Tribune
Chicago Tribune
Cincinnati Enquirer
Indy Star
Albany Times Union
Buffalo News
Richmond Times Dispatch
Daily Gazette
Chart Attach Toronto
Cleveland Beakon Journal
Washington Herald
Palm Beach Post
Go Memphis
Deseret News
Salt Lake Tribune
Seattle Times
Sacticket
Wilkes-Barre Times Leader
Orange County Register
LA Times

TELEVISION AND WEB ARTICLES

"Clay Aiken Is No Longer Invisible." CBS News, July 7, 2004

Lini Markowski, Bonnie. "In Defense Of Clay Aiken Fans Everywhere." TV Reality Calendar, July 6, 2004

Austin, Diane. "Clay Aiken-Revisiting The Profile And Power....MichNews.com July 5, 2004

Elber, Lynn. "Clay Aiken Ready To Light Fuse On Holiday Concert, Tour." Comcast.net June 30, 2004

Kirkwood, Kyra. "Catch Clay." Redlandsdailyfacts.com, February 18, 2004

Rogers, Steve. " '*American Idol*' Continues Setting Ratings Records With Tuesday Broadcast." Reality TV World. February 4, 2003

Cameron, Dean. "Aiken Finally Getting His Due." Newmusiccountdown.com, Janury 13, 2003

"Clay Aiken Bobble Head Night Set For January 10." nineronline.com, December 15, 2003

Macquire, James. "The Clay Aiken Grammy Controversy." About. Com, December 12, 2003

Vick, Justin. "UNCC Officials Say Aiken Received No Special Treatment." nineronline.com, December 9, 2003

"UNCC Charlotte May Prosecute Students Who Scalp Graduation Tickets." WSOC.com, December 3, 2003

Berkley. "Clay Aiken Reality Check: Reflections On A 6 Months Career." Assistant Director Of Motion Pictures and Screen Writer, November 2003

Ruggieri, Melissa. "Two 'Idols' MIA" timesdispatch.com, January 22, 2003

Daniel Fienberg. "Clay's Aiken For Actin. Zap2it-TV News, January 22, 2004

Sprague, Diane. "Taken By Surprise." Beavers On Idol, January 20, 2004

Barker, Bruce. "Idols Soar, Music Industry Sneers." Foxes On Idol," November 25, 2003

Hafizah, Osman. "Clay Aiken: Boy-Next Door Turns Chart Topper." Channelnewsasia.com (Singapore), November 20, 2003.

Potts, Kimberly. "Vandross Scores At AMAs." Add Entertainment-E! November 17, 2003.

Davis, V. "Clay Aiken: He Came, He Sang, He Conquering." Guest Commentary, November 4, 2003

O'Reilly, Bill. "Extreme Media." Bill O'Reilly.com, October 23, 2003

Moss, Cory "Aiken Makes A Big Scene In New Video" MTVAsia. Com October 14, 2003

Brown, Carolyn. "Revenge Of The Nerds." Msnbc.com/news, October 10, 2003

"Interview with Clay Aiken." pbskids.org, October 2003

"One Day Chart Topper: Aiken's Taking Over." hitsdailydouble.com, October 16, 2003

Diers, James. "She's Not That Innocent About Image." MSNBC, October 10, 2003

"Triumph Of The Nerds." ABC.com, October 9, 2003

Brown, Carolyn. "Revenge Of The Geek Heartthrob." MSN.com, October 10, 2003

Reynolds, Donna. "Update: Kimberly, Clay, and More!" Foxes On Idol September 29, 2003

Courtright Jr., Ray. "*American Idol* Tour Review." Elites TV, September 1, 2003

Sochacka, Sherry. "Does The Winner Take It All?" Foxes On Idol, August 9, 2003

"Music Manager Not Idle After Idol." Clear Channel News, August 7, 2003

Staff Writer. "On Amazon Chart, Clay Is No. 1." Charlotte.com, July 5, 2003

Macquire, James. "This Week's Hits: Where Is Clay Aiken?" Top 40/Pop, July 4, 2003

"Aiken's Album Follows Path Of Single-Straight To No. 1." wral.com, July 4, 2003

Shepherd, James. "Is Clay Aiken A True Idol?" Beavers On Idol, July 13, 2003

Kaufman, Gil. "*American Idol* Ruben Studdard is Lucky He Has A Healthy Ego," July 14, 2003

Moss, Cory. "Clay Aiken's 'Night' Video Says 'This Is The Soul'" MTV, July 12, 2003

Macquire, James. "Take The *American Idol* Poll: Clay Aiken, Kelly Clarkston or Ruben Studdard?" Top40/Pop July 1, 2003

"Harry Potter And The Idol Of America." Lycos 50, June 24, 2003

Bloomberg, David. "Marilyn vos Savant Tackles The AI Voting Issue." Foxes On Idol, June 23, 2003

Calloway, Volanda. "Claymania Continues With Release Of CD". Wral.com, June 10, 2003

The Associated Press. "Aiken Beating Studdard In Record Sales." WSOCTV.com, June 2, 2003

Macquire, James. "This Weeks Hits—Clay Aiken, Superstar." Top40/Pop.

Sochacka, Sherry. "From Idol To Icon." Foxes On Idol, May 29, 2003

Schman, Andrea. "You Say Tomayto, I Say Tomahto: The Clay Conspiracy." Foxes On Idol, May 16, 2003

Courtright Jr., Ray. "Musical Idol Beyond The *American Idol* Competition." ElitesTV, April 2, 2003

Ausiello, Michael. "Scoop! Ruben/Clay Rematch Scratched." tvguide.com, April 1, 2003

OTHER SOURCES:

Staff—A.E. Finley. YMCA Raleigh, North Carolina

Laxton, David. Director Of Communications—Autism Society Of North Carolina.

Gaye Deamer

Bonnie Wallace

Photo Loaned By Bonnie Wallace

INDEX

PRODUCTS ORDER FORM

Easy access orders: www.PublishingHouse.biz (Gives product descriptions.)

Fax orders: 801-294-9776

Postal orders: Publishing House P.O. Box 540508   No. Salt Lake, Utah 84054-0508

Please send the following books: (Prices are subject to change.)

$21.95-Clay Aiken: Everything You've Ever Wanted To Know About The Singing Sensation.

$19.95-Commercial Foods Exposed! And How To Replace Them.

$12.95-Help! Help! It's Egg Momelet

$12.95-Wallpaper Cookies

$12.95-Polka Dots and Paint

-Parent's And Kids Say, "No More!" (Forthcoming)

Name:_____
Address_____
City:_____State_____Zip_____
Telephone:_____
e-mail address_____
Sales Tax: Please add 6.50% sales tax.

Shipping: U.S: $4.00 for first book and $2.00 for each additional product. International: $9.00 for first book; $5.00 for each additional product (estimate).

Payment: Check   Credit Card (Do not send cash.)

Visa   Master Card

Card number_____

Name on card:_____Exp. Date_____